An amazing journey

The Church of England's response to institutional racism

A report on the development of the Committee for Minority Ethnic Anglican Concerns (CMEAC), the former Committee on Black Anglican Concerns (CBAC)

A personal perspective by
Glynne Gordon-Carter

CHURCH HOUSE
PUBLISHING

Church House Publishing,
Church House,
Great Smith Street,
London SW1P 3NZ

ISBN 0 7151 3855 3

GS Misc 702

Typeset by Vitaset, Paddock Wood, Kent
Printed by Cromwell Press Ltd,
Trowbridge, Wiltshire

Published 2003 for the Committee for Minority Ethnic
Anglican Concerns of the Archbishops' Council by
Church House Publishing.

Copyright © Glynne Gordon-Carter 2003

This report is dedicated to my devoted mother, Mrs Violet Eulalee Gordon, teacher and headteacher, who was a strong person and well-respected in the communities in which she lived and served in Jamaica. She instilled in me many positive values, such as commitment, honesty, respect for other people, discipline, (the importance of doing one's best) and the value of a good education.

I leave you Love
I leave you Hope
I leave you the challenge of developing Confidence
In one another
I leave you a thirst for Education
I leave you respect for the use of Power
I leave you Faith
I leave you – Dignity

Engraving on a statue of Mary McLeod Bethune, prominent educator and social reformer – to be found in Lincoln Park, Washington DC – whose words these are.

Contents

Contents

Figures

Message

I had the very great privilege of working as a colleague with Glynne Gordon-Carter. Following the publication of *Faith in the City* it was manifestly clear that the Church of England had a long and difficult journey to travel in tackling racism within its own life. Glynne's arrival and subsequent work for the national Church helped us get on the road and start to face and tackle the issues. Her own Christian faith, life experience and professional integrity gave depth and wisdom to the endeavour. We owe her a very great debt.

✠ John Gladwin
Bishop of Guildford

Preface

Valuing cultural diversity is built on the principle of photo-tropism. Just as plants are attracted towards the light, so valuing people's culture has the same effect, that of ensuring health and growth. This means taking the best from the past to build a better today for a brighter tomorrow. Any attempt at mere tolerance of other cultures will not do; and the theory of making English culture a melting pot for other cultures is doomed to failure. The issue is one of respecting, appreciating, and enjoying other cultures. And the critical issue for minorities and their cultures is not one of lacking self-esteem but of lacking cultural esteem.

Glynne Gordon-Carter's *An Amazing Journey* charts the way in which this growth was nurtured amongst minority ethnic Anglicans through the work of the Committee for Minority Ethnic Anglican Concerns. Sometimes the growth was blighted by the coldness of the Church's response – as in the rejection of the motion designed to ensure an increased participation by minority ethnic members through their election to the General Synod. But as Glynne and others have persevered in the task, there is now more cause for rejoicing as new fruits of the work are beginning to be seen in our church communities across the country.

This has indeed been an amazing journey, a mixture of joy and despair, struggle and achievement. As Glynne looks back in this report over the troughs and peaks in the landscape of the past 15 years, she picks out some of the landmarks of our experience, not only in order to reflect on the route we've come, but to point the way forward for the steps of those who will follow.

To take just some of these:

- *Seeds of Hope* and its sequel *The Passing Winter* have had a tremendously positive effect which must continue to be taken forward in our Eucharistic communities. Awareness of its concerns and findings, and the good practice which is being developed, must become part of our life as Christians together.

- Minority ethnic Anglicans must be encouraged by their communities of invited guests of Jesus Christ, and be nurtured and supported to stand for election to the PCC, Deanery Synod, Diocesan Synod and Bishop's

Councils, and the General Synod, to ensure that there is proper participation at every level of the Church's governance.

- The encouragement of our young people to be included and valued at every level of church life is a key element of our call to be Good News to the whole of our communities.

- The development of vocations amongst minority ethnic Anglicans is a challenge which must be taken up and pursued with vigour. Glynne's own story of how she was encouraged in her application for the position she held for 14 years is a model of how the church can help its minority ethnic members to take that vital step. And she prays daily for the best which is yet to be.

- There are many more: equal opportunities schemes, ethnic monitoring, mentoring schemes, awareness raising in our schools – rural as well as inner-city; the education of our prospective ordinands in their colleges and courses.

But the work must be properly resourced. Glynne often struggled against the lack of will to provide proper funding and adequate staffing for the huge task. And, as Philip Giddings said in his presentation of *Called to Lead*, 'Words are not enough; it is action that is needed, action which has a demonstrable, visible effect upon our church life … what we are engaged upon is a process of achieving deep-seated change, change within ourselves as well as within our Church.'

That we are accountable for what we do and what we are – that in spite of all aids or hindrances from without, each soul is the cause of its own happiness or misery – is a truth certified to us both by Nature and Revelation. As Martin Luther King said, 'We shall have to repent in this generation, not so much for the evil deeds of the wicked people, but for the appalling silence of the good people.'

So, let us rejoice in this history of what has been done so far, but resolve with all our hearts to ensure that the work is continued and supported so that our church will truly demonstrate our understanding that we have a shared humanity, a membership of One World. We need other human beings to help us to be human. We are made for interdependence, for complementarity. We are made for family, the human family, God's family. Let us make sure that we value every member of it.

✠ John Sentamu
Bishop of Birmingham

Foreword

I frequently lament the way black people's contributions in so many fields of human endeavour have been written out of history, and I am convinced that this is no accident. In addition, I frequently urge black people to record, for the assistance of future historians, what their experiences have been, and deplore the lack of such records. It may be that in reading the manuscript of this book for the purpose of this foreword, I have stumbled on the reason.

Mrs Gordon-Carter describes the going-on in General Synod when the only one of 63 recommendations in the *Faith in the City* report rejected by Synod's Standing Committee, and consequently by Synod itself, was the recommendation for a Standing Commission on Black Anglican Concerns; and later Synod's rejection of the proposal for a minimum number of 24 black members in a Synod of almost 600. I found that in reading her account I was reliving all the pain I felt at the time – the rejection by people who professed to respect and even admire me, but clearly believed that more people like me constituted a threat to them and theirs. The pain has not diminished over the years.

We all owe Mrs Gordon-Carter a great debt for this chronicle, and I personally owe her more than most. After the behaviour of General Synod's Standing Committee, I carried on as Chairman of CBAC only because I was 'a man under authority' and was also appreciative of the late Archbishop Runcie's genuine concern. But all this was not happening in a vacuum. At that time we were having spectacular examples of police mistreatment of black people even in their own homes; at work, in the schools, in the shops, on the streets overt and covert reminders to black people that we were in the society but not of it, were commonplace. It was clear to me that as expressed by Synod's behaviour, Church of England members saw Christianity not as the local expression of an universal faith, but as the religious expression of their national identity – and this was white.

Glynne Gordon-Carter's arrival was little short of miraculous. Too recently arrived in Britain from the Caribbean not to be shocked at what she was seeing and hearing; a track record of successful strategic planning and organization building; and deep faith in the good purposes of God which was not dependent upon popular acclaim, she was also blessed with a pleasant personality and shrewd judgement of human character. She was not going to be deterred in her brick-making because little straw was forthcoming! It was her appearance on the scene which more than anything else encouraged me 'to gird up my loins and face the journey to Horeb' (1 Kings 19).

✠ Wilfred Wood
November 2002

Acknowledgements

It is important to acknowledge the significant and positive influence which General Synod (GS) debates on reports such as the British Council of Churches' (BCC) report entitled, *The New Black Presence in Britain: A Christian Scrutiny* (1976), together with the Board for Social Responsibility's (BSR) Report on *Britain as a Multi-Racial and Multi-Cultural Society* (1977) have had in raising the awareness of members of the General Synod. An analysis of this debate, together with a succession of debates on topics such as the Special Projects Fund of the BCC's Community Race Relations Unit, spearheaded chiefly by the Board for Social Responsibility, and based on BSR reports published between 1977 and 1984, have been provided by the Revd Canon Clarence Hendrickse in his MPhil. thesis entitled, *General Synod's Response to Racism as a Factor in the Church of England's Maturation as a National Church.*

I would like to acknowledge the work which was done by the Revd Kenneth Leech in his role as BSR's Race Relations Field Officer between 1980 and 1986. He travelled extensively across the dioceses and parishes in order

> to educate church members and congregations so that they could make an informed Christian response and contribution to a multi-racial society based on a plurality of cultures and religions; and in that context to develop means of promoting the Projects Fund of the Community and Race Relations Unit of the British Council of Churches.[1]

The impressive amount of work which was done by the Revd Leech and the Race and Pluralism Community Group on behalf of the Board for Social Responsibility was invaluable as it helped the Board to guide the church in the next phase of the work. The Revd Leech felt that

> whatever happened in the future, it seemed clear that a central focus of any work must be that of confronting racism within the thinking and structures of the Church. Judgement must begin at the house of God.[2]

The report and recommendations from the Leicester Consultation on *The Church of England and Racism* held in 1981 and the Balsall Heath Consultation on *Anglicans and Racism* held in 1986 (both organized by

BSR), also contributed towards the drawing up of priorities for the Church of England's task in combating racism. The recommendations from the Archbishop of Canterbury's *Faith in the City: A Call for Action by Church and Nation* (1985) gave ample guidance by stating three clear objectives to be achieved if the Church was to 'make a clear response not only to racial discrimination and disadvantage, but also to the alienation, hurt and rejection experienced by many black people in relation to the Church of England'; also the structures which should be set up and staff to be appointed to serve those structures.

I would like to express my sincere appreciation to the members of the Committee for Minority Ethnic Anglican Concerns (former CBAC) with whom I worked over the years from 1987 to 2001. Here I need to mention especially the Chairmen: Bishop Wilfred Wood, Bishop John Sentamu, and the Revd Rose Hudson-Wilkin (current Chair). I worked with three different committees and I felt supported by many committee and sub-committee members, namely: Canon Ivor Smith-Cameron (the first person to call and congratulate me when I was appointed to the post!); The Ven. David Silk, former Archdeacon of Leicester, now Bishop of Ballarat in Australia, Mr Mark Birchall, Bishop Colin Buchanan, the Revd Rajinder Daniel, the Revd Prebendary Theo Samuel, Mrs Gloria Rich, Mrs Hazel Simmons, the Revd Charles Lawrence, the Revd Canon Clarence Hendrickse, the Revd George Kovoor, Mr Justin McKenzie, Mr Deo Meghan, Mrs Vinnette Melbourne, Mrs Beverley Ruddock, Mrs Dorothy Stewart, Miss Cynthia Sutherland, Ms Smitha Prasadam, Mr Ralph Straker, Miss Josile Munro, Captain Rayman Khan and Miss Anne-Marie Parker. Shortly after my appointment, Bishop Tom Butler, who was at the time Bishop of Willesden, invited me to a welcome supper and to meet a group of black Anglicans. I would also like to record my thanks to the members of the Diocesan Network (Diocesan Link Persons and 'Joynt Hope' members), and the members of the small Support Group; as well as members of various CMEAC sub-committees. Several members of staff were very helpful to me, namely: Bishop John Gladwin (my first boss in Church House); Mr Richard Hopgood, Director of Policy and my Supervisor; my secretaries – Misses Romilly Leeper, Gillian Bloor, and Mrs Bernadette Marren, who was more like an assistant; The Secretary Generals, Sir Deryck Pattinson and his successor, Mr Philip Mawer; the staff of the Board of Education, the Board for Social Responsibility, the Communications Unit, Church House Publishing and the Print Room; and other staff of General Synod's Boards and Councils, especially those who assisted with various projects.

Over the years the contribution made by many people towards the development of CMEAC's work has been a wonderful blessing and harnessing of talents and experience. It is with great humility that I express sincere gratitude to everyone for their genuine support which inspired me especially when there were difficult times, and gave me hope to continue in my task of developing the Committee's programme of work. I was able to build up a network of support at the centre, in the dioceses and, at the national level. I was also in contact with my counterparts internationally: the Revd Canon Dr Harold Lewis, ECUSA Officer for Black Ministries, and his successor the Revd Lynne Collins and the Revd Laverne Jacobs, Co-ordinator, Council for Native Ministries, Anglican Church of Canada. It is impossible to name everyone individually but those who have not been named are of no less significance in the time which they gave and the contributions which they made to the development of the Committee's programme of work.

This report which chronicles the development of the Committee's work has taken up a great deal of time during the first year of my retirement. However I felt that my work would be incomplete without this record as the Committee was breaking new ground in challenging the Church of England to combat institutional racism in its own structures. Canon Hendrickse's thesis was invaluable and saved me several trips to the Record Centre – many thanks Clarry.

I am very grateful to Bishop John Gladwin, Bishop John Sentamu, Bishop Wilfred Wood and Canon Ivor Smith-Cameron for the interviews I had with them. They supported me in my idea to write this report. I am also grateful to Bishop John Gladwin for the title of this report – while interviewing him he commented on the development of the work as being an amazing journey.

I would like to acknowledge the contribution of Mrs Bernadette Marren in typing some of my early attempts. Miss Juliet Lopez came to my rescue in Trinidad and patiently and cheerfully typed the full report. She saw it through several drafts! I also wish to express my sincere thanks to Miss Sarah Roberts and her colleagues in Church House Publishing who meticulously guided me through the procedures involved with publishing this report.

Last, but by no means least, I would like to thank my friends and family who had to hear about the work and listen to my gripes from time to time; heartfelt thanks to Gilbert Carter, my husband, who supported me in his quiet, consistent manner, taking me to the coach station at an ungodly hour each morning in all types of weather, having to fend for himself while I was away at countless overnight and weekend conferences, and being good humoured about it all. He also encouraged me to pursue the MSc degree in Race and Ethnic Relations at London University and taught himself the computer in order to undertake the typing of all my assignments. Once again he came to the rescue and painstakingly edited this report. Gilbert's attitude helped me to bear the load lightly.

The Committee's work was demanding and called for creativity, vision, energy and enthusiasm, it was a big challenge and I felt privileged to be a part of it.

Summary

In December 1987, I was appointed to work as Secretary to the Board for Social Responsibility's Race and Community Relations Committee (RCRC). Also, I was seconded to work for the Committee on Black Anglican Concerns (CBAC), which was redesignated the Committee for Minority Ethnic Anglican Concerns (CMEAC) in 1996.

The RCRC was to be a new permanent committee properly integrated into the Board's structure. The RCRC's main task would be 'to carry forward the work begun and established by the Race, Pluralism and Community Group of BSR and its Field Officer, the Reverend Kenneth Leech'. Consequently, the range of work to be done by the secretary would be in keeping and building on the pioneering work which he had done. 'The Committee had primary responsibility within the Board for matters of national policy on issues of race and community relations, especially in relation to racial justice and racial harmony'.[1]

The Committee devoted its attention mainly to issues such as immigration, education, employment (especially related to the high level of unemployment among young black people), housing and black people in the criminal justice system.

With respect to the CBAC, the Secretary of RCRC's main area of responsibility would be

> to advise it on all substantial issues affecting the needs and concerns of Black Anglicans. The expectation is that this committee will be challenging the Church of England to make whatever changes are thought necessary in its life and organization to respond to the experience and concern of its black members.[2]

I was meant to be the eyes and ears of CBAC in terms of what black Anglicans were saying and experiencing in their church life and to assist the Committee in developing strategies to help the structures of the Church of England combat institutional racism.

Whereas RCRC was meant to be a permanent committee, CBAC was to be 'established for an initial period (perhaps five years), with a review towards the end of this term leading to a decision on the need for an extension of its life'.[3]

The importance of the job was underscored thus: 'The general purpose of the job is to assist the Board for Social Responsibility and, through the Committee on Black Anglican Concerns, the whole organisation of the General Synod to respond to the issues of race and of racism in our society'. The Job Description stated: *we are conscious that the task to be done is daunting and the journey to be undertaken by the Church of England in these matters is considerable* (my emphasis). The CBAC was accountable to the General Synod (GS) Standing Committee.

By 1990, it became obvious that my task was not only daunting but almost impossible because of the growing volume of work and the expectations of both committees. The situation was reviewed by the General Synod's Standing Committee which took the decision to appoint me full-time to work for the Committee on Black Anglican Concerns. This meant that the Committee could redouble its efforts to work with the structures to combat institutional racism.

Unfortunately that decision resulted in the resignation of the Revd Stanton Durant, Chairman of RCRC, who was angry and disappointed at what had happened. He felt that since the Church of England was not prepared to support the work, then he would resign from the committee and from the Board for Social Responsibility. The Revd Durant also felt that decision was not keeping faith with *Faith in the City* which had stated: 'This would not require the establishment of a new post but rather for the Synod to fund the whole (rather than 50 per cent at present) of the BSR's work in this field.' During the next few years, the RCRC's programme of work was held in abeyance although various aspects were undertaken by BSR staff as their schedules permitted.

The CBAC's work to combat institutional racism in the Church of England was being developed, while the Roman Catholic Church was conducting its own programme with the promotion of the publication *With You in Spirit* (1986), the Methodist Church had set out its agenda arising out of its reports entitled *A Tree God Planted* (1985) and *Faithful and Equal* (1987). The Baptists and URC denominations, as well as the Quakers were also developing their programmes. The denominational staff gave each other invaluable support and I was fortunate to be part of that ecumenical team which worked with the British Council of Churches' Community Race Relations Unit as I served on its board and some of the unit's sub-committees. I also served as one of their representatives on the Executive

Committee of the Churches' Commission for Migrants in Europe based in Brussels, as well as the Council of European Churches' Racism and Xenophobia Working Group.

This report presents the development of the Committee's work from a personal perspective, in my role as Secretary to CBAC, and subsequently CMEAC, from 7 December 1987 to 31 October 2001. It chronicles the development of the Committee's work from 1987 to 2001 and holds up a mirror to the Church of England at the beginning of the twenty-first century. It shows the impact which the committee has had on the national, as well as the diocesan structures in working with the Church of England to combat institutional racism and it documents the role of the Archbishops' Council as it leads the way on how the church should respond to the Stephen Lawrence Inquiry Report. The report also identifies factors which hindered progress, as well as factors which contributed towards the development of the work. In pointing to the future, the report will identify further 'Seeds of Hope'.

The CBAC's theological framework is set out in Section 2, Chapter 4. I will not deal with the use of appropriate terminology in this report as the *Seeds of Hope in the Parish Study Pack* devotes a section to definitions. Suffice it to say it is important for the Church of England to be contemporary in the use of language as it relates to 'race' issues, for instance words such as: 'coloured', 'half-caste', 'non white' are not appropriate.

Definitions

The Church of England has accepted the definitions for racism and institutional racism from the Stephen Lawrence Inquiry Report (1999).

Racism

Racism in general terms consists of conduct, words or practices which disadvantage or advantage people because of their colour, culture or ethnic origin. In its more subtle forms it is as damaging as in its overt form.

Institutional racism

Institutional racism is the collective failure of an organization to provide an appropriate and professional service to people because of their colour, culture or ethnic origin. It can be seen or detected in processes, attitudes and behaviour which amount to discrimination through unwitting prejudice, ignorance, thoughtlessness and racist stereotyping which disadvantages minority ethnic people.

It persists because of the failure of the organization openly and adequately to recognize and address its existence and causes by policy, example and leadership. Without recognition and action to eliminate such racism it can prevail as part of the ethos or culture of the organization. It is a corrosive disease.

Part 1

Introduction

chapter 1
Background

The message that was generally percolating through to the children of the mother country was that their labour was wanted, not their presence.[1]

The main thesis of the New Black Presence report is that in Britain there is a problem caused not by black people, but by the nature of British society and features of that society which have been present long before the recent phase of black immigration ... In a brief historical survey it suggests that the nature of the relationship of British people with black people in Britain had been conditioned by slavery, colonisation, trade and mission conducted in Africa and Asia.[2]

Before presenting the work of the Committee on Black Anglican Concerns, it is necessary for me to provide background information so that the reader can understand the historical context out of which this work came, and why it was necessary for the Church of England to set up a committee within its structures to work with the church to combat institutional racism.

In the British West Indies, the slave trade was the indispensable handmaid of the sugar industry and in the eyes of the British colonial masters sugar was established as 'king'. It is estimated that between 1651 when the English slave trade to the West Indies started, and 1808 when it was abolished, approximately 1,900,000 slaves were taken into the British West Indies. It is thought that during the whole European Transatlantic slave trade (Portuguese, British, Dutch, French and Spanish involved) no less than 20,000,000 Africans were sold out of Africa – a quarter of whom were taken to the West Indies. It must be stated that these figures were for arrivals after hazards of the transatlantic crossing and do not include those who were killed during collection in Africa, those who jumped overboard, or who died on the long sea voyage.[3]

On arrival in the West Indies, families, tribal and linguistic groups were split up as the planters feared slave rebellions. For the most part, slaves had to hide to practise their religious and cultural customs. The result was that their ancestral African cultures were virtually destroyed by slavery and colonialism. Even names were changed as the slaves acquired a version of British culture still evident, for instance, in the Jamaican dialect – patois, which is spoken alongside Standard English. In the very rural areas of Jamaica patois is practically the only language spoken.

With respect to education during slavery, three-quarters of planters' children came to England for their schooling.

During the 18th century in Britain, education was left mainly to the home and to charity, and schools were founded by benefactors. This tradition was also practised in the West Indies. Christopher Codrington left two Barbados plantations and some slaves for founding a college to teach medicine and theology, and in 1735 Harrison College was founded for twenty-four indigent planters' children. In Jamaica, Wolmers, Mannings, Ruseas and other schools owed their origin to similar bequests. There were similar stories in Trinidad and other territories. These were all grammar schools.

The enslaved part of the plantation received an education of a sort. Newly arrived slaves had to be 'seasoned' – that is, they had to be given time to adjust themselves physically to their environment. They learned their work under the direction of a driver who was one of the trained slaves. The trades were taught by craftsmen brought from England. The purpose of training was to get as much value in labour as possible from the slave. Only the missionaries thought that slaves should be taught to read and write. In 1797, the Barbados Consolidated Slave Act made it the duty of every Anglican vicar to set aside a time every Sunday for instructing the slaves in the doctrines of Christianity, but it was illegal to teach reading and writing. Through the Moravians, Methodists, Baptists, Anglicans, Roman Catholics and Presbyterians, in course of time after Emancipation, schools were introduced.

With respect to education in the colonies, the Church and the British Government worked in partnership. Two years after the British Government gave its first grant for elementary education in England, it gave £25,000 for the education of West Indian people, and further grants were made up to 1846. Beyond a doubt the churches bore the main burden of organising education and establishing schools, while some of the West Indian governments assisted with small grants.[4]

There were serious deficiencies in the quality and context of education up to the 1970s. Technical and Vocational Education were poor relations, and

West Indian History, West Indian Geography and Literature were not taught. My first exposure to West Indian History was at the University of the West Indies where I gained a degree, after which I took the opportunity to apply for a teaching post in Trinidad, where Dr Eric Williams, Prime Minister, and an outstanding historian, had started a drive to recruit teachers of West Indian History. Those of us who graduated in 1965 were proud to be the first graduates of the University of the West Indies and not graduates of the University College of the West Indies, which had been an affiliate of the University of London. In 1998, the University of the West Indies celebrated its fiftieth anniversary through its main campus in Jamaica, the campuses in Barbados and Trinidad, and extra mural centres in other former British territories in the West Indies.

It was mainly through the Church of England that Britain left its mark on religion and education in the former British territories, as the Church was part of the colonial superstructure; apart from civil servants and defence personnel, priests were also sent to the British islands.

Whether in the Catholic or Anglican colonies, priests were poor in quality and never enough to minister even to the whites. The Church in Europe was at a low ebb and the clergy who offered to go to the colonies were not the most devoted. Some clergy became planters, merchants and in one case the commander of a privateer fleet. Like the planters some clergy were against the conversion of slaves. Yet others were respected for their sincerity, good works and learning.

The Society for the Propagation of the Gospel (SPG) which was founded in Britain by Thomas Bray in 1701 had as one of its aims: 'the instruction and baptism of African Slaves who were being brought to work in North America and the Caribbean, in order to affirm their humanity if not their freedom'. The bequest of the Codrington Estate to SPG meant that the Society was very involved with the founding of Codrington College in Barbados.

> Mary Howard and Mrs Reid were employed in 1797 at Codrington College to give instructions to slave children and to teach them to read … Today USPG is a major mission agency of the Anglican Church in Britain and Ireland. The organisation works in partnership with Anglican and United Churches in more than 50 countries exchanging people and resources.[5]

By the end of the eighteenth century, all the churches inspired by the religious revival had started missionary organisations. The Anglican Established Church, itself had been stung to some action in the field in

1794, when it set up the Society for the Conversion and Religious Instruction and Education of the Negro Slaves in the British West Indian islands. The Baptist and Missionary Societies were founded. The Moravians were the first comers ... in 1756.[6]

Apart from the obstacles which the missionaries experienced with the slaves, the planters were opposed to their presence. Note the instructions which were given to Anglican missionaries.

You must be careful ... to give no offence either to the Governor, to the Legislator, to the Planters, to the Clergy or any other class of persons in the island. They were to prove first of all that a man could be a good Christian, and a good slave at the same time ... It was the idea of brotherhood in Christian teaching which seemed so dangerous to the planters. The missionaries were to all intents and purposes saying for the first time that a European was the 'brother' of a Negro Slave ... Laws were passed to cut down the activities of missionaries. With the non-conformist missionaries as their teachers in Sunday school, the Bible became the holy book of the slaves.[7]

The publication entitled *Staying Power: The History of Black People in Britain* by Fryer records the presence of Africans in Britain before the English came here. They were soldiers in the imperial army which occupied the southern part of the island for three and a half centuries. Fryer remarked that black people (meaning Africans and Asians)

had been born in Britain since around the year 1505. In the seventeenth and eighteenth centuries, thousands of black youngsters were brought to this country against their will as domestic slaves. Other people came of their own accord and stayed for a while or settled here. By the mid-eighteenth century, approximately 10,000 black people lived in Britain. They were mainly household servants, pages, valets, footmen, coachmen, cooks and maids – much as their predecessors had been in the previous century. Some of the black performers in the seventeenth century were Asians. Like the African slaves in Britain, Asians were sometimes ill treated, and Asian slaves were sometimes advertised for sale ... Associated in many English people's minds with the immense riches of Africa and India, and the immense riches amassed by the West and East Indies, black servants conferred on their masters and mistresses an air of luxurious well-being. They were at once charming, exotic ornaments, objects of curiosity, talking points, and above all symbols of prestige ... Free Asians occasionally advertised their availability for work.[8]

By the nineteenth century, communities of black people began to establish their homes in the dockland areas of ports such as London, Liverpool, Cardiff and Manchester. It is recognized that Liverpool has the longest history of Chinese settlers in Britain.

chapter 2

Post-war Britain

Their British passports gave them the right to come to Britain … the 'Motherland' offered them a gleam of hope.[1]

Although black people had been living in Britain for centuries, the year 1948 marked a large-scale black immigration to Britain from the Caribbean. In this paper the term 'black' refers to people of African, Asian or African-Caribbean descent. The term 'black' is also used to refer to any one who is subject to racial discrimination on the basis of skin colour. This is a socio-political usage of the word.

In 1998, the fiftieth anniversary of the arrival of the SS Empire Windrush from Jamaica to Britain was commemorated. In the publication entitled *Forty Winters – Memories of Britain's Post-War Caribbean Immigrants,* Sam King comments:

> As we got closer to England there was great apprehension on the boat because we knew the Authorities did not want us to land. I got two ex-RAF wireless operators to play dominoes outside the radio room on the ship so we could keep informed of the messages coming in. We heard there was consternation in Parliament and that newspapers like the *Daily Graphic* and the *Express* were saying that we should be turned back. It was a Labour Government and the Colonial Secretary Creech-Jones that said, 'These people have British passports and they must be allowed to land'. But then he added, 'There's nothing to worry about because they won't last one winter in England.'

King added, 'It gives me some satisfaction to be able to repeat his words forty winters later.'

The majority of people who came on the Windrush, as well as others who arrived in later years from the Caribbean, Asia and Africa were responding largely to a call for manpower in post-war Britain, as there was a desperate shortage of labour in this country; added to that, many came to get away from high unemployment and low wages in their respective territories. However, it must also be noted that a small number came to study, mainly in the legal and medical professions, and return to home. One of my uncles travelled on the Windrush to Britain, studied law at one of the Inns of Court in London and returned to Jamaica. In the 1980's Justice ROC White retired as a high court judge. Nurses were recruited from British Guyana and other Caribbean territories. Fryer commented, 'A Tory Health Minister (Enoch Powell) welcomed West Indian nurses to Britain.' Interestingly, in October 1999 while visiting Trinidad I noticed an advertisement in the *Trinidad Guardian*, from the WorldWide Health Care Exchange advertising for nurses from Trinidad and Tobago. The advertisement read, 'Have you ever thought of working in England? We will be travelling to Trinidad in October with the South Manchester University Hospital. Many exciting positions available. Give us a call for further information or send us your resumé.'

In the 1950s and 1960s, London Transport recruited from Barbados, Trinidad and Jamaica. In some cases, their fares were paid by their employers and subsequently deducted from their wages. Other major employers, including British Rail, also introduced similar programmes. London Transport's direct recruitment continued until 1970. When Pakistan and India became separate states after Independence, many were looking for a life free from the famine and miserable poverty which was their countries' chief legacy from imperial rule. The tiny community of settlers from the Indian sub-continent began to grow as rural workers from India and Pakistan came to work in Britain, again with official encouragement. There were strong incentives to take advantage of their right to settle in Britain.[2]

Post-war immigrants in Britain helped to fill vacancies mainly in manufacturing, transport, health, hotel and the restaurant industries. On arrival in Britain, black people experienced a great deal of racial discrimination in their daily lives, in employment, and in housing where the sign 'no blacks, no Irish, no dogs' was commonly displayed. They also suffered racial discrimination in education, the criminal justice system and health, as well as in the social services.

The Church was no exception: black people experienced racism in the traditional denominations whether they were Roman Catholics, Methodists, Baptists or Anglicans. In the case of the Church of England, some people had been card-carrying Anglicans and had arrived in Britain with recommendations from their rectors.

> Having come from countries with such a high proportion of church attendance, it would be natural to suppose that a first inclination of the newly arrived immigrants would be to seek out a church. The Church it may be thought would provide the natural link between them and the

community into which they had moved ... The Church would provide the one 'known' among a multitude of unknowns.[3]

In the Foreword to *Seeds of Hope: Report of a Survey on Combating Racism in the Dioceses of the Church of England*, Bishop Wilfred Wood, the first Chairman of the Committee stated:

> Some descendants of these slaves arrived in Britain in the 1940s, '50s and '60s from the Caribbean. Other people of colour arrived at the same time from Africa and the Indian Sub-continent. For the most part, these newcomers from the Caribbean were Church of England born and bred, who could sing from memory many hymns from the English Hymnal and Hymns Ancient and Modern, not to mention the canticles at Morning and Evening Prayer Services, and also the Anglican chants. In the Caribbean, they were used to worship in a Church where the clergy and leadership were English and white, and so anticipated nothing but acceptance and even welcome in churches in Britain, with whose liturgy they were thoroughly familiar. They were disappointed. The racism they encountered in a society which denied them adequate housing, jobs for which they were qualified, and reasonable services and credit facilities, was also present in the Church. Clergy from the Caribbean returning to England on furlough or on retirement, were dismayed to find erstwhile faithful members of their flocks not in Anglican congregations, but either reading their Bibles at home or members of 'Immigrant' house churches, which eventually became the predominantly black independent churches that took root, and now play an important part in the life of our society.

The Church in Jamaica was under the control of the Diocese of London. In 1998, the Mothers' Union in the Diocese of Jamaica celebrated its centennial anniversary. This was the first Mothers' Union to be established outside of England. In 2000, St George's Anglican Church in Kingston, Jamaica (our family church) celebrated its one-hundred-and-seventieth anniversary.

In his book entitled *West Indian Migrants and the London Churches,* Clifford Hill provides figures on the total Christian community in the British Caribbean around 1955. These were as follows:

- 897,000 Anglicans
- 155,700 Baptists
- 30,500 Congregationalists
- 155,615 Methodists

- 29,916 Presbyterians
- 808,500 Roman Catholics
- 390,454 Other Denominations.

Hill said that churches were well attended and of the West Indian migrants who settled in London, 69 per cent attended traditional churches in the Caribbean. After migration to London only 4 per cent continued to attend such churches. There were several reasons for this massive fall-off in church attendance after migration: coming to Britain was itself a secularizing experience – there was pressure to work long hours, shifts, and Sundays; secular or profane alternatives to church-going were more attendant; the weather was cold and churches were empty; but not least racism in church was a potent ingredient in the stew of reasons for the massive lapse.

Wilkinson, in the publication entitled *Inheritors Together* (1985), gave examples of people being told by the vicar that they should not return to worship at that church, as the congregation would not approve. One woman remarked: 'The first year of attending church they ignored you, the second year they ignored you, the third year they asked you to buy a raffle ticket.'

Ample testimonies have been provided by people who came to Britain from the Caribbean in the publication entitled *Cold Arrival: Life in a Second Homeland* (1998):

> I recalled in the early days turning up at places and being told we are not letting any of you in tonight. I had a similar experience in the church.

> On the first and second Sunday we were made welcome. On the third Sunday we were met at the door and told to make our visits less frequent. We got the message and did not return.

> In the Caribbean, the church had always been a central part of our lives – spiritually, educationally and socially. In Britain, we were disillusioned to find the churches unwelcoming, and in some cases even embarrassed by our attendance. We were made to feel intruders in God's house.

My experience of rejection is similar. In 1992, my husband and I went to live in Milton Keynes. On the first occasion that we attended the Church of Christ the Cornerstone, at the end of worship we were welcomed by a worshipper who sat next to us. She asked whether we were visiting Milton

Keynes. We explained that we had just relocated to live there. When we told her where we were living, she stated that in that vicinity there was a Pentecostal Church. Although Christ the Cornerstone is ecumenical she could not envisage that we could belong to any of the five denominations – URC, Methodist, RC, Baptist or Church of England!! This lady was the wife of one of the clergy.

Despite the rejection which they experienced, many black people had been christened and confirmed as Anglicans so they decided to remain in the Church of England. They had a strong Anglican identity and had no desire to worship anywhere else, as many were Anglican from birth. The idea of belonging was strongest among the people from the Caribbean – Christian, English-speaking and brought up in the British education system, they found it very difficult to come to terms with the prejudice of British society. The Swann Report quotes a West Indian mother:

> Many of us came here with a myth in our minds, the myth of belonging. We have also raised our children to believe that they belong in these societies and cultures (simply because they were born here) only to find that as they grew older, they were seen in the eyes of the host community as a new nation of intruders. Our children are then faced with great traumatic and psychological problems, since they are made to feel that they do not belong here, also they feel that because they were not born in the West Indies they do not belong there either.

The survey of black Anglicans carried out in the 13,000 parishes of the Church of England, which the Committee conducted with the help of the Statistics Department, found that there were 27,000 black worshippers, and more black than white families took their children to church. More will be said about the survey later in this report.

Bishop Peter Selby, in his book entitled *Belonging: Challenge to a Tribal Church,* is concerned with the kind of community the Church is called to be. '... the Church has to have a different way of being community from that which we see in other human communities. The longing of God is for the entire created order to be transformed into the harmony and beauty for which it was made.'[4]

Bishop Selby said that his intention was to seek a different kind of analysis and to propose that issues of longing and belonging arose constantly within the Church and needed to be faced again and again. In the chapter entitled 'An Ethnic Church?' he analysed the 1989 General Synod debate on the motion which the Committee had brought before the General Synod with respect to the need to ensure that a larger number of black Anglicans got elected to the Synod. His thought-provoking critique is very well worth reading. Bishop Peter said that those who were opposed had been at great pains to say that they were not motivated by any lack of desire to have more black members. They believed that it was the act of introducing ethnic monitoring and affirmative action into the Synod's electoral processes that was racist and discriminatory.

All the speakers agreed that within the Church of God there should be no question of ethnic distinction. All should be treated as persons, without reference to their colour of their skin or their country of birth. Indeed, it was evident that the variety of people's ethnic origin was for some speakers too awful even to contemplate, let alone mention. The making of special provision for people of minority ethnic groups would be something to which, as one speaker averred, 'no black man (sic) I know – and I have lived among them for a large part of my life and know many – who is worth his salt' would wish to be party. *So it seems that to make special provision for the election of black people is patronising; to speak on their behalf is not* (my emphasis).

We are thus invited to believe that membership in the Body of Christ does not so much include or transcend our ethnic and other differences as obliterate them. Our Christian membership is as discrete individuals, cut off from cultural roots and social background which have made us what we are and which might constitute a significant part of what we have to offer to one another. *All sorts of gifts can accompany us into the Church, but not those that come with our ethnic origin* (my emphasis).[5]

Bishop Selby goes on to comment that:

In other areas of its life the Church does not shrink from attending to people as members of distinct groups. Archdeacons and legal officers, universities and cathedral all have special privileges of representation.[6] … What was being defended therefore was not the aim of democratic processes but a particular way of doing things, and doing things our way is precisely what ethnicity is about … It is a constant tendency of dominant ethnic groups to assume that ethnicity occurs only in minorities. Chinese, Indian or Caribbean cooking is often described as 'ethnic', while fish and chips are not![7] … In the ethnic behaviour of dominant and majority groups there is this double forgetting: there is the forgetting of the humanity of those who are pushed to the margins, and there is the forgetting of the experiences of exclusion and marginalization in the dominant group. Yet memory is not all that is suppressed in a refusal to change processes that exclude others from participation. When we consent to situations that keep others down we are suppressing not just memory but also hope.[8]

In her book entitled *The Dream of God: A Call to Return,* Verna Dozier, a leading black theologian is critical of the Church as an institution, she begins her publication with a quote from the Book of Common Prayer.

Gracious Father, we pray for thy Holy Catholic Church. Fill it with all truth, in all truth with all peace. Where it is corrupt, purify it; where it is in error, direct it; where in anything it is amiss, reform it. Where it is right, strengthen it; where it is in want, provide for it; where it is divided, reunite it; for the sake of Jesus Christ thy Son, our Saviour.

When asked by a very intelligent and learned man what her book would be about she replied,

It's going to be about how I think the institutional Church has missed the mark of what it ought to be about.
'The institutional church?' he puzzled, 'What other church is there?'
'The people of God', she replied. 'The baptised community.'
'But how would they function without an institution?' he smiled.
Aye, there's the rub, as Hamlet would say. The little band, the church of St. Paul's day needed an organisation, a structure, an institution to maintain itself, but the institution took over the little band.[9]

Dozier remarks, that the only reason for her to write a book about how the Church has failed to be what it is called to be, is to hold up again the vision of what it is called to be in the biblical story – the dream of God. The institution has missed its high calling because we, the people, have missed ours. Christians, during the time of their becoming a structure among other structures of the world, distorted the call by turning it into institution.

Part 2

Alienation, hurt and rejection expressed by black Anglicans

chapter 3

Faith in the City: A Call for Action by Church and Nation

> There has been a widespread recognition in the evidence submitted to us that racial discrimination and disadvantage still represent a challenge to be overcome in society. There were calls for the Church of England to respond by stressing the importance of compliance with the present laws against direct and indirect discrimination.[1]

The *Faith in the City* (FITC) report of the Archbishop of Canterbury's Commission on Urban Priority Areas (ACUPA) was launched in 1985. Among other issues, the report documented the alienation which black people were experiencing in the Church based on evidence given by black Christians, as well as the Commission for Racial Equality (CRE). The CRE said in their submission:

> Members of minority ethnic groups who, for the most part, feel left out of the mainstream of British society, felt equally ignored and relegated to the peripheries of church life. Many black Christians told us that they had felt 'frozen out' of the Church of England by patrician attitudes. Some had left the Church, yet others were still solid Anglicans. We have heard repeated calls for the Church of England to 'make space' for and so better receive the gifts of black Christians.

Faith in the City expressly stated:

> There needs to be a clear lead from the centre. We believe that organisational changes must be made at national levels to facilitate progress with these and other issues. We believe that the Church must make a clear response not only to racial discrimination and disadvantage, but also to the alienation, hurt and rejection experienced by many black people in relation to the Church of England. FITC recognised the primary need for national and diocesan policies to be particularly sensitive to the needs of minority ethnic groups.[2]

The report identified complementary initiatives which should be taken in relation to General Synod bodies: the Board for Social Responsibility, the

Advisory Council for the Church's Ministry (ACCM), and the setting up of the Commission on Black Anglican Concerns. The report stated that 'any one of those initiatives on its own would be desirable, but not necessarily sufficient'.

FITC gave three objectives to be achieved:

1. that the issues of racial discrimination and disadvantage are given a clearer and more sustained emphasis in all that the Church says and does;

2. the promotion of a greater awareness of these issues, and associated socio-cultural aspects, throughout the Church;

3. the removal of barriers to the effective participation and leadership of black people at all levels of church life, particularly in relation to ordained ministry.

Also, it was made clear that for those objectives to be met: 'structural changes would need to be effective, in terms of the process of management and policy implementation, and accountable within the Church structures and in relation to the black Anglican constituency.'[3]

Staffing

The *Faith in the City* report recommended the appointment of three members of staff in order to manage the proposed initiatives in BSR, ACCM and the Commission on Black Anglican Concerns. This was not granted.

Later in this report I will comment on the resourcing of the work.

Commission or committee?

The FITC's recommendations included: 'the establishment of a wide ranging, *Standing Commission* on Black Anglican Concerns which should be established for a minimal period (perhaps five years) with a review towards the end of this term leading to a decision on the need for an extension of its life'. The Report also recommended that 'this Standing Commission should have one full-time staff officer based in the General Synod Office and have right of access to meetings and papers of the Boards and Councils of General Synod'.

The Standing Committee of the General Synod recorded their view of the setting up of a Commission in GS 715. They were not yet convinced that the establishment of a Standing Commission on Black Anglican Concerns was the right way to achieve the goals and aims reflected in paragraph five of FITC.

In the General Synod debate (February 1986), the Revd Canon Ivor Smith-Cameron spoke on his amendment to the Standing Committee's opposition: 'My amendment proposes that we need to work out details in consultation with the Boards of the General Synod (and especially ACCM and BSR) – for the establishment of a Commission on Black Anglican Concerns.'

The General Synod narrowly rejected his amendment by 207 votes to 197, with 17 abstentions. In view of the closeness of the vote on this amendment, an understanding was given that the Standing Committee would consider the matter further.

A second Report was presented at the 1986 November Synod (GS 753) in which it was recommended that a *Committee* on Black Anglican Concerns should be established with the status of a Sub-Committee of the Standing Committee. This was passed. Canon Smith-Cameron expressed his disappointment to General Synod. 'This decision of an all-white Standing Committee not to recommend a Commission for Black Anglican Concerns had sent a wave of bewilderment, distress, frustration and horror throughout black constituencies, both in the Church and in society outside the Church.'

The Standing Committee had opposed the motion because it believed that the establishment of a Commission would not help the cause of unity in the Church. There was also a concern about how it would relate to the rest of the church and whether the work would be marginalized. In his thesis, Canon Hendrickse stated:

> there was an underlying feeling within the Standing Committee that groups of black people meeting together might become subversive … the fear in Synod flowed from the idea of a group of black people coming together and having the power to officially criticise the values, attitudes and modus operandi of Boards or Committees in their negative effects on black church members.

It must be clearly noted that FITC had recommended a *Commission*; this was rejected by the General Synod on the advice of the Standing Committee; and instead a *Committee* was agreed. Added to that, instead of appointing a full-time staff officer, part of the time of a member of the Secretary General's staff, and part of the time of the BSR's Race and Community Relations Officer would be assigned to the CBAC.

chapter 4

The Committee on Black Anglican Concerns (April 1987–March 1991, the early years)

There is nothing sacrosanct about present *mechanisms* of democracy; the important thing is for those mechanisms to give an effective franchise and voice to all sections of plural society.[1]

It follows therefore that in any forum which genuinely seeks meaningful black participation, there can be no substitute for the presence of black people. I use the word *participation* advisedly, and I would draw your attention to the fact that this is the word used throughout this report in preference to *representation*.[2]

The Right Revd Dr Wilfred Wood, Bishop of Croydon (the first black Bishop in the Church of England) was appointed to chair the Committee, which held its first meeting in April 1987. Members included representatives from the following bodies: the Standing Committee, ACCM, the Board of Education, the Board of Mission and Unity (BMU), BSR, the Central Board of Finance, black Synod members, the Association of Black Clergy, and House of Bishops' nominees. Also CBAC had the power to co-opt four members. The Committee was mixed in ethnicity; however, most of its members were from the minority ethnic community, in keeping with the Committee's Constitution and Membership attached as Appendix 1.

Terms of Reference

The principal tasks of the Committee on Black Anglican Concerns will be to monitor issues arising, or which ought to arise, in the context of the work of the Standing Committee, the Central Board of Finance and the Synod's Boards and Councils, and of the General Synod itself; as far as they have policy implications for minority ethnic groups within the Church and the wider community. The Committee is asked to pursue its work in close collaboration and partnership with the bodies concerned and their staffs, reporting in the first instance to the

Standing Committee and, as appropriate, to the General Synod. As a second responsibility, the Committee is asked to report to the Standing Committee not later than 31 December 1989 on the experience derived from its first three years work and on the provisions which it considers would be appropriate to make for Black Anglican Concerns in the General Synod of 1990/95.

Appendix 2 provides a list of members of that first Committee which served from April 1987 to March 1991. The Association of Black Clergy, which had first conceived of the idea of having a body to address black Anglican concerns, was very involved through its representatives with the setting up and work of CBAC. In its early meetings, the ACUPA Advisory Group (assigned to follow up FITC) devoted a great deal of time to assisting with the implementation of the proposals for the setting up of CBAC.

Increased black membership in the General Synod

From its inception in April 1987, the Committee understood that one of the major issues to be tackled would be the under-representation of black people within the synodical structures. This would be in keeping with the agreed principal task of the Committee, that is, monitoring of issues arising, or which ought to arise, in the context of the Boards and Councils of Synod, as well as Synod itself.

Faith in the City had specifically recommended that the new Synod to be elected in 1985 should consider how a more appropriate system of representation which pays due regard to minority interest could be implemented for the General Synod elections of 1990.[3]

The Committee spent nearly one year discussing this issue as a Committee and also in dialogue with the Standing Committee and the Policy Sub-Committee on how this could be achieved. For fifteen years there had been only two black members serving on General Synod with a membership of over five hundred, the Revd Canon Ivor Smith-Cameron and Mr Vijay Menon. By 1985, there were six black members of General Synod and the idea was to seek to increase this number to twenty-four.

This number was chosen to ensure black representation on Synod's Boards and Councils without a too small number being over burdened (1988; Proceedings, Vol. 19 (3), p. 1103). At that time there were no figures available to indicate the level of black membership within the Church of England, and in any case was thought to be irrelevant to achieving the desired objective. The number 24 was more arbitrarily than statistically based. FITC had referred to a figure of 4 per cent for the black population, which was derived from the 1981 Census. However, it was felt that was an underestimate of the black population in England.[4]

The Committee's strategy for the 1990 General Synod Elections would be to encourage as many black people as possible to stand. If there was a shortfall then under the powers of the proposed Measure, the two Archbishops in consultation with the Prolocutors of Canterbury and York, and the Chairman and Vice Chairman of the House of Laity would have the power to make up the number to 24 from those who had been close runners up but had nonetheless failed to be elected.

The outline principles which the committee proposed for amendments to Canon H2 and the Church Representation Rules, would include an ethnic monitoring questionnaire. Many General Synod members were opposed to this idea for various reasons. The question of ethnic monitoring would surface again through the Southwark Diocese and into the General Synod for consideration, debate and decision by the end of the century.

In the November 1988 GS sessions, the Standing Committee presented a Report on *Black Membership in the General Synod* – GS 844. This was supported by GS 844a, *A Report from the Committee for Black Anglican Concerns*. In addressing the General Synod, Bishop Wilfred, as Chairman of the Committee, laid emphasis on *participation* as against *representation*:

It follows, therefore, that in any forum which genuinely seeks meaningful black participation, there can be no substitute for the presence of black people. I use the word *participation* advisedly and I would draw your attention to the fact that this is the word used throughout this report in preference to 'representation'. Parliament, Local Government, Trade Unions, Clubs and democratic institutions may order themselves on the basis of *representation* and, therefore, talk of quotas, lobbies, majority votes, etc. may rightly be applied to them. But I should have no need to remind this Synod that the Catholic Church of Jesus Christ is like nothing else on earth, or anything else that the world has ever known. Because what Empire, Nation, Parliament, Borough Council has there ever been where the supreme motivation in all things and all times is meant to be *love*? And what institution is there whose members derive their sense of worth from that claim 'while we were yet sinners Christ died for us' and they, therefore, lay claim, not to *rights* but to privileges? My sisters and brothers, we serve the secular world ill if we take our cue from them and so order the life of the Church on the same patterns they have devised in deference to power. We would fail to offer them a model of participation and fellowship made workable by respect and love.

Archbishop John Habgood, Archbishop of York, was invited to move the substantive motion, generally endorsing the proposals and asking for the preparation of the necessary instruments. As part of his presentation the Archbishop said,

> I am sure that the Synod is aware that it faces both a problem and an opportunity. The motion before us is an attempt to grasp the opportunity ... But if in the end it means going to Parliament, then to Parliament we must go and on Parliament must fall the responsibility of rejecting what we put forward. We must not be deterred at this stage.

The General Synod gave a three to one majority vote in favour of the proposal to increase black membership in Synod. This was very good news, not only to the committee but to many members of the Church of England – black and white, as well as to those outside the Anglican community. The Synod debate in November was seen as a watershed:

> we believe that many black Anglicans recognised it ... As a corporate expression by the Church of a readiness to begin the process of addressing in specific and practical ways some of the issues identified in *Faith in the City*.

However, because of Section 25 of the Race Relations Act 1976, Counsel advised the General Synod that a Measure would be required if they decided not to request the Home Secretary to make an Order according to Section 73 of the Act.[5]

Such a Measure was drafted (GS 866X), debated and lost at the February Group of Sessions 1989. The result of the vote was as follows:

- House of Bishops voted 17 in favour and 3 against
- House of Clergy voted 103 in favour and 62 against
- House of Laity voted 80 in favour, and 96 against

The vote to give general approval to the draft Synodical Government (Amendment) Measure was lost because the House of Laity voted against it. Some members of the Standing Committee played a critical role in speaking and voting against the Measure. In fact the request which was made to vote in Houses was like the 'kiss of death'. There was an overall majority (200 to 161) votes in favour of it, but the successful call for a vote by Houses meant that it had to pass in all three; and although the Bishops and clergy both supported it substantially, it fell through an adverse vote of 80 to 96 in the House of Laity.

Mrs Penny Granger, Standing Committee member told the *Church Times* that she was very concerned that the whole Measure was flawed and that while the Synod was trying to do the right thing, it was going about it in the wrong way. The responsibility for what happened did not rest only with her. It rested also with the 24 other members who had supported her call for a vote by Houses and with the 95 other members in the House of Laity who had voted against the Measure.

Reaction to the debates and final vote

The result of the debate caused many Anglicans and people from the wider black community to be quite disillusioned. CBAC members were distraught and bewildered at the Standing Committee's attitude.

The Measure had been controversial and the laity in particular were unhappy with it and powerful speakers were mustered against it. Not one black member of GS was invited to speak. In the November 1988 debate there had been a willingness to accept the Committee on Black Anglican Concerns' analysis of the difficulties which needed to be overcome in order to increase the number of black people in Synod. By February 1989 there seemed to be a reaction against such acceptance, members preferring to make judgements on personal anecdotal evidence, and values and attitudes more reminiscent of British Empire and colonial days. When the Archbishop of York finally intervened to answer the charge that the draft measure was patronising because it ought not to be the kind of help black people should want, he said: 'We are being patronising if we say "Ah, but this is not what the black community really wants, we know better because we met somebody out in Africa some 20 years ago and that isn't what he thought"'.[6]

After the 1988 debate, there had been

a great sense of euphoria following the acceptance of the principle of increased black representation... the strength of feeling against the Measure in February 1989 caught many by surprise. Not even the intervention at the end of the debate by the Archbishop of York, and the Archdeacon of Leicester, neither of whom had intended to speak in the debate, could save it.[7]

In the aftermath, the Committee on Black Anglican Concerns, in a note to the General Synod's Standing Committee, stated:

> The effect of the Synod's failure to give general approval to the *Synodical Government (Amendment) Measure* has been severely to damage, if not indeed to destroy, the trust and confidence of black Anglicans in the Synod's commitment to *Faith in the City* particularly as regards the bringing of black people into full participation in the life of the Church at all levels.

CBAC felt that the signals which had been sent by the General Synod in February, meant that it would be impossible to encourage black people to stand for the elections. In fact, some members of Synod were considering resigning from General Synod. The Committee itself came close to resigning.

Many white members of General Synod commiserated with committee members and CBAC's secretary in the corridors of Church House after the February debate. Bishop Wilfred found the rejection of the Measure 'very sad indeed'. It showed, he said 'that there were Synod members who were still trapped in the "Christian slave owners" thinking: like them they wanted black people to be happy, but under the conditions they provided and without requiring any adjustment of their own comfortable state'. Bishop John Sentamu said, 'It was an opportunity missed and a set back for the whole Church and the debate had shown the inability of many members to hear what was being said.' In her article entitled 'Rebuffs to the Blacks' in the *Church Times*, Margaret Duggan spoke about the scarcely veiled racism of some of the speakers in the debate. She stated further:

> The Church like the Police keeps paying lip service to the need and desire for many blacks to come forward for training to take their rightful place as leaders in the community. But once more the Church in action seems to have slapped them in the face. It is very important that Synod works quickly to find some way to convince them that that is not what was meant.

Several people wrote to console CBAC and to suggest a way forward. The ACUPA Advisory Group chaired by Bishop Tom Butler, wrote to the Archbishop of Canterbury about ACUPA's concern and regret that 'the General Synod failed to carry through in February the decision it took in principle in November to ensure more adequate representation of black Anglicans'. He stated that the Advisory Group was 'anxious that a way forward should be found and fairly quickly, before people took up hardened positions'.

The Diocesan Race Group chaired by the Revd Peter Hawkins wrote to the Secretary General as representatives of the Church working among the black communities of dioceses. The letter stated:

we feel we must pass on to you the deep dismay and frustration felt by many black people at the recent defeat of Measure GS866X which was designed to increase black membership of Synod.

We find that vote to be devastatingly out of tune with the principle expressed in 'Faith in the City' (5.74) that present systems of democracy are not sacrosanct and must not prevent us giving an effective voice to all sectors of our plural society.

The Diocesan Race Group urged members of the Standing Committee to seek ways to redress this wrong.

Attendance at both debates was my first encounter with the General Synod. I was shocked to hear the appalling speeches which were made by some members. It was a painful experience. I remember looking around the gallery on more than one occasion to see whether there were other black people listening to the debate and thanked God that there were just a handful of us. I was dismayed at the level of ignorance which was being displayed by some members of the General Synod. It was clear that the committee would have an immense task to educate the Church to understand the nature of racism, and the role of the Church as an institution in combating racism within its own structures.

In my opinion, Bishop Wilfred's speech was masterly, but I am not sure whether General Synod members wanted to hear the stark truth. The tension in the Chamber was palpable. Members were either strongly in favour of, or definitely against the Measure. On leaving the Chamber at the end of the debate, a senior member of General Synod asked me whether Bishop Wilfred had written his speech![8]

For weeks after the February debate, I felt disenchanted and disillusioned and wondered whether I could be inspired to continue as the Committee's Secretary. For me, the turn around came as a result of attending a Celebration in Birmingham at the NEC on Saturday, 22 April 1989. Archbishop Desmond Tutu was the specially invited guest. The theme for the day was 'Freedom to the Oppressed'. It was inspiring to hear Archbishop Tutu preach and to meet him after the service. The Archbishop's words to me were something to the effect: 'so you are the lady who Bishop Wood tells me is working in the church to combat racism'. He autographed my copy of his biography written by Shirley du Boulay with the words 'Glynne, Thanks for your splendid ministry. God Bless.' I was thrilled and felt uplifted!

Both Archbishop Runcie, as well as Archbishop Habgood were very concerned about the 'fall-out' from the February debate. The Archbishop of Canterbury acted promptly by requesting a meeting with CBAC within one week of the General Synod debate. The Archbishops also held meetings with the Committee on Black Anglican Concerns, as well as representatives from the Standing Committee at Lambeth Palace. Appendix 3 provides a copy of the letter and press release which was sent by Archbishop Runcie, Archbishop of Canterbury to Bishop Wilfred Wood.

In a resolution, the Standing Committee stated its regret that the failure of the Synodical Government (Amendment) Measure

> should have attributed to the severe alienation, hurt and rejection experienced by many black people in relation to the Church of England and affirmed its conviction that there should be fuller participation by black people in Synodical Government at all levels, including the General Synod, its Boards and Councils.

After a great deal of deliberation, CBAC agreed to continue with its work but made it quite clear that it would assist but could not lead in the process of encouraging greater participation by black people in General Synod.[9] The Chairman of the House of Laity of General Synod, with the encouragement of the Archbishops and the General Synod Standing Committee, invited the Chairmen of the Diocesan Houses of Clergy and Laity respectively to separate meetings in the Autumn. The main purpose of the meetings was to discuss the importance of seeking a secure and greater level of participation of black people. Appendix 4 provides the full text of a letter which was sent by Mr Deryck Pattinson, Secretary General, to Diocesan Bishops. Both meetings were well attended. Discussions centred around the presence of black Anglicans within the Church; and the role of Chairmen in identifying, supporting and assisting black people for the 1990 General Synod Elections. 'As part of the programme of awareness, the House of Bishops requested Diocesan Bishops to hold meetings in their dioceses with their Lay and Clerical Chairmen and one black representative'.[10]

The role of Archbishop Runcie and Archbishop Habgood in acting quickly to retrieve this situation was impressive as their personal intervention helped to diffuse the situation. On at least two other occasions in quieter times the Committee was invited back to Lambeth Palace by Archbishop

Runcie, Archbishop of Canterbury, and in later years by his successor, Archbishop George Carey.

The strategies which were put in motion to rescue matters were carried out through the Standing Committee, in conjunction with the Committee on Black Anglican Concerns and Diocesan Bishops. This included the development of a network of black Anglicans across the dioceses whose task it would be to do the following: to assist in making contact with key people in the dioceses for their support in preparation for the General Synod Elections; to encourage black Anglicans to come forward for the 1990 General Synod elections and to help in their preparation. The CBAC Diocesan Network was developed with the help of the Diocesan Bishops who nominated the Link Persons to represent their dioceses. Twenty-two dioceses were represented at the first meeting which the Committee hosted on Saturday, 9 December 1989.

The *Living Faith in the City* report (1990) in reviewing what progress had been made in the Church towards combating racism since the publication of *Faith in the City* stated:

> We therefore make no apology for saying that the elections to General Synod for 1990–1995 and the participation and success of black candidates in the process will be of crucial importance in demonstrating just how far the church has really grasped the message from *Faith in the City*.[11]

The Committee also felt that the 1990 General Synod Elections would be truly a litmus test. Fourteen black members were elected as noted in the analysis in Appendix 5.

The journalist Betty Saunders commented in the *Church Times*, 'There are at least 14 black Anglicans in the recently elected General Synod, 7 of them new members. They are the fruit of a successful campaign born out of bitterness and anger.'

The General Synod Election Pack

> When speaking at Synod, less is more. If you are elected, before you speak at General Synod, prepare what you are going to say. Say something worth listening to and do not attempt to major on every subject. Be patient, precise and do not ramble! Take your time and be reflective.[12]

In preparation for the 1990 General Synod, the Committee had prepared an election pack to be used by black candidates as a tool. The pack gave helpful advice for the campaign, the importance of good preparation, tips on writing the electoral address, how to handle the press, the hustings, the GS structures, and how to conduct oneself if elected.

The pack was to be used for future elections. It was revised for the 1995 GS Elections with the help of some black members of GS and CBAC. The text for the 2000 pack was revised with the support of successful candidates from the 1995 GS Elections. Miss Anne-Marie Parker, a volunteer with the Committee, designed the graphics which made it more reader-friendly and attractive.

The pack was distributed through the committee's networks, and at the request of some bishops copies were made available to other candidates in several dioceses. The Committee was very pleased about that development.

It has always been essential to start planning for the GS elections well in advance and so the revision of the pack is usually done one year in advance of the elections for printing 'in house', and circulation. Candidates have found the pack useful in terms of giving vital information. I hope that the candidates for the 2005 GS elections will benefit from an even more improved pack. The idea is really that the pack should be kept up to date so that its relevance is unquestioned and it continues to be an invaluable aid. Hopefully this 'easy to read' information pack will serve as an incentive for more minority ethnic people to consider putting themselves forward for the elections.

Contact with General Synod's boards and councils

In keeping with the Committee's Terms of Reference '... to monitor and to make recommendations about issues which arise or ought to arise in the context of the work of the Synod's Boards and Councils, as far as they have implications for minority ethnic groups within the Church and in the wider community', as part of its programme on an ongoing basis the Committee invited the Chairman and Secretary of each General Synod Board and Council to attend one of the CBAC meetings.

Invitations were issued several months in advance and the main objective was to collaborate with each Board on issues of concern to CBAC, as well as issues of mutual concern. With each new quinquennium it was necessary to arrange such meetings as new Board/Council Chairmen were appointed.

Over the years, the Committee has held several meetings with the Board of

Education (mainly in relation to church schools), the ACCM (especially in relation to vocations, the setting up of the Simon of Cyrene Theological Institute, also ethnic monitoring of applicants and ordinands), and the Board for Social Responsibility (especially in relation to BSR's racial justice work which was carried out through the Race and Community Relations Committee and subsequently through the Community and Urban Affairs Committee). Also the Committee held meetings met with representatives of the Board of Mission, the Council for Christian Unity, and the Central Board of Finance.

This concept was extended to include invitations to Sir Richard O'Brien, Vice-Chairman of the Church Urban Fund (CUF) with whom the Committee raised its concerns about funding to minority ethnic groups. Several years later, Mrs Angela Sarkis, Chief Executive of CUF was invited to attend a CBAC meeting. The Archbishops' Appointments Officer, the Clergy Appointments Adviser and the Church Army Vocations Officer also accepted invitations to attend committee meetings.

I hope that every effort will be made by the present Committee to continue with this strategy, as this initiative has proved beneficial in the following ways:

1. Helped the Committee to open up dialogue and discussion with Boards and Councils regarding their role in working to combat institutional racism.
2. Created a better climate of understanding.
3. Often led to opportunities for collaborative work.
4. Helped to establish the Committee's work within the national structures.
5. Served as a lever to remind Boards and Councils of the importance of inviting black members of GS to serve as Board or Council members.
6. Meetings provided the opportunity for frank discussion in a challenging yet non-threatening manner.

During my first few weeks in Church House I decided to set up appointments to meet with Board/Council Secretaries. This was in order to introduce them to the work, introduce myself as a new colleague and provide the opportunity to discuss areas of collaboration as I quickly realized that I needed to liaise with other senior staff in Church House.

In one case as I walked into the room for my appointment, I was greeted with the words: 'What is this about wanting to meet with me? Don't you know that in Church House people just get on with their work?' Being new

I didn't quite know how to interpret that but I did not let that deter me or dampen my enthusiasm.

The Committee's theological framework

The theological framework of the Committee's work is threefold:

1. *The nature of God*; one God, a Trinity in unity; a God of justice and mercy.
2. *The nature of humanity*; men and women of every hue and ethnic group belong to the one human race; are all made in the image of God, and each is of unique worth in his sight.
3. *The nature of the Church;* a people called into being through the sacrifice of Jesus Christ to be a community of reconciliation, love, justice, and sharing a foretaste in our time of God's eternal kingdom.

God is shown in Old Testament and New Testament alike as opposed to all forms of injustice and exploitation. The law sets out what his love and justice requires; the prophets call God's people to recognize how far they are falling short. God is shown as particularly concerned for the needs of the 'fatherless and widow, the alien or stranger within your gates' (Deuteronomy 10.18 and 19), that is to say, for all those who for any reason are less able to stand on their own feet. Jesus underlines the prophets' call for justice and mercy in his teaching, and demonstrates it in his attitudes and actions.

But slavery and colonization (inter alia) have distorted the encounters between people of differing ethnic groups, and left a legacy where black people have for centuries experienced injustice, discrimination and exploitation in various forms at the hands of white people. So today black people in the UK still are subject to excessive economic and other disadvantages, as almost all official 'statistics of deprivation' confirm. It would be surprising if this seepage from our national life did not find its way into the Church, and its cancerous potential for the whole life of the Church must not be underestimated. Racism is a sin.

The God of justice and mercy challenges his people to put right things that are wrong within the community of faith. Black people have known rejection within the Church itself for several generations especially during the 50s and 60s (painful memories of this are still around at a deep level); in many places still there is only tolerance where there should be welcome and appreciation. Worse still many white Christians seem not to hear the black voice as it articulates the inbred deference, pain, desires and aspirations of black Christians. Some of the speeches at the February 1989 General Synod debate on the draft Synodical Amendment Measure (GS 866), which proposed a minimum of 24 black members of Synod, revealed that such attitudes are still far too widespread in the Church.

The God of love calls his people, both in Old Testament and New Testament, to be a community within which our common humanity is recognized, all man made barriers are broken down (all are sinners, saved only by God's grace; Ephesians 2.8–18); all share the gift of his Holy Spirit without distinction of age, sex or skin colour (neither Jew nor Greek, neither slave nor free, etc., Galatians 3.28; and how Jesus related to those rejected by 'religious' people). The Church should be a community marked by love and reconciliation within itself, demonstrating and also proclaiming the same love and reconciliation to the world.

It is a serious contradiction of this proclamation when within the fellowship love is withheld: when a common faith and baptism are seen to be of less importance than colour and kith and kinship, and the world outside can see clearly that the Church is not living up to its own professed character.

The doctrines of creation and redemption, law and grace all challenge the behaviour of the Church. Its failure in the past may be due to ignorance, blindness, or even to the fact that many find it difficult to relate easily to those who they perceive as 'different' – whether the difference is colour, class, culture or gender. But failure it is.

Further, many have failed to see that real reconciliation requires the sort of repentance, which by God's grace bears tangible fruit. Where things have been wrong, positive steps need to be taken to put them right. Repentance without such action is bogus.[13]

As the preoccupation with the Synodical Government (Amendment) Measure and its aftermath subsided, the Committee was able to turn its attention to other, though no less important, matters.

The setting up of the Simon of Cyrene Theological Institute

Under the leadership of the Revd Canon Dr Sehon Goodridge, now Bishop of the Windward Islands, West Indies, the Institute was opened in Autumn 1989, and inaugurated in April 1990 by Archbishop Robert Runcie, at a memorable service held at St Anne's Church, Wandsworth. Bishop

Goodridge had been Principal of Codrington College, Barbados before assuming the position as Principal of the Institute. The Institute was to offer courses for pre-theological training of ordinands and accredited lay workers. It would also provide placements and pastoral studies units for white and black candidates in training for ordination at theological colleges and courses belonging to the churches who participate in the Institute. The Board of Governors was ecumenical in its make up.

The proposal to establish a centre for the study of the black religious experience had originated from the Association of Black Clergy, and several Association members were keenly involved in the planning and management of the project; to name a few: the Revd Barry Thorley, the Revd Rajinder Daniel and the Revd John Metivier. Clergy from other denominations were also committed to this project. The Revd Brian Russell, ACCM's Secretary to the Committee for Theological Education, was specially assigned to be involved with the financing, planning, and development of the Institute. The Diocese of Southwark gave premises in Wandsworth and grants were provided through charitable trusts. The General Synod gave financial assistance.

CBAC was very supportive of the Institute and assisted in different ways, such as with the design of the Lay Leadership Course. In 1990, the Principal was invited to attend the CBAC's 1990 residential meeting in order to speak about his vision for the Institute; the Committee also invited him to address a luncheon hosted for General Synod members. CBAC members were very pleased about the opening of the Institute which had materialized after many months of planning and discussion. The Revd Rajinder Daniel and Mr Justin McKenzie served as CBAC representatives on the Board of Governors. CBAC's third place was made available to the Appointments Sub-Committee which appointed Mr Mark Birchall (GS member to serve on the Board of the Institute).

Bishop Goodridge served as Principal for approximately four years. He was succeeded by the Revd Amos Kasibante. Unfortunately, due to a variety of factors the decision was taken to close the Institute. This decision was not taken lightly. There was a great deal of discussion about its future spearheaded by Mr Philip Mawer, Secretary General, representatives of the Advisory Board of Ministry (ABM) the former (ACCM), and Bishop John Sentamu. The closure of the Institute has been a big disappointment for many black Anglicans, as well as white Anglicans who had benefited from the courses on offer. (The plan is that the Institute will be re-established in a different setting.) The General Synod is willing to offer financial support in order to ensure its rebirth. The Diocese of London is playing a key role in the setting up of the new study centre.

Ethnic monitoring of applicants and ordinands

The ACCM decided that it should be part of their acknowledged policy that everyone who was eligible as a candidate for professional ministry would receive equal treatment at selection level whatever his/her colour or ethnic or national origin. CBAC was consulted and assisted ACCM with preparing a letter and an ethnic monitoring questionnaire. This has become established over the years. Consistency in the provision of the figures to the Committee on an annual basis should be encouraged. The Committee has made efforts to encourage ethnic monitoring of Readers. More will be said about ethnic monitoring later in this report.

Equal Opportunities Policy (EOP)

From its inception, CBAC was very keen that Church House should set an example to the dioceses by formulating and implementing an Equal Opportunities Policy. The Central Board of Finance prepared a draft EOP as the employing authority for the staff at Church House and the Committee was asked to comment on it. CBAC responded and requested that the Committee should be consulted further before the terms of any statement were issued, also that CBAC should be involved in the process of monitoring the policy. The policy was 'put on hold' for a number of years because there was uncertainty about how sexual orientation should be handled. More information will be provided about the development of the Equal Opportunities Policy later in this report.

Relationship with the General Synod's Standing Committee

The Committee on Black Anglican Concerns was constituted as a Sub-Committee of the Standing Committee which received its minutes and had to approve any reports which the Committee wished to publish. As stated under its terms of reference, CBAC was required to report to the Standing Committee by the end of 1989 with recommendations for the General Synod of 1990/95 (see pp. 20–21).

The General Synod agreed that if the Committee's Chairman was a member of the General Synod, he would be free to attend meetings of the Standing

Committee and to take a full part in its business though he would not be free to vote. At the time of his appointment by the Presidents, as the Chairman, Bishop Wilfred Wood, was not a member of the General Synod. Accordingly, the Committee requested Canon Ivor Smith-Cameron, GS member and member of CBAC, to represent the Committee at the Standing Committee meetings. Canon Smith-Cameron proved to be a good representative.

The failure of the Draft Synodical (Amendment) Measure had resulted in a great deal of distrust by CBAC towards the Standing Committee, not least because before going to the Synod, the Committee had discussed its proposals with the Standing Committee at length. A note to the Standing Committee in March 1989 set out clearly the views of CBAC and the seriousness of the situation.

> What we were not prepared for was the number of members of the Standing Committee who voted against the general approval motion … We think it is disgraceful that the call for a vote by Houses should have come from a member of the Standing Committee.

CBAC raised questions about the Standing Committee's relationship with it and asked what course of action the Standing Committee had in mind.

> We see the responsibility now as resting with the Standing Committee given its position within the Synodical system and its particular contribution to the creation of the present unhappy situation.

As reported earlier the Standing Committee invited CBAC to attend its March meeting which then led to a second meeting. This in turn led to a meeting at Lambeth Palace between the Archbishops, the Standing Committee and CBAC. Although 'mending of the fences' had begun, I felt that the trust between CBAC and the Standing Committee was never fully restored. The Committee lived up to its responsibilities as a body accountable to the Standing Committee and the Standing Committee was mostly supportive of the Committee's work.

By 1990, in keeping with its terms of Reference the Chairman of CBAC presented a paper to the Standing Committee on the experience derived from its first three years' work and on the provisions which it considered would be appropriate to make for Black Anglican Concerns in the General Synod of 1990–95. CBAC's Terms of Reference were revised with the approval of the General Synod Standing Committee in January 1990, as presented in Appendix 6.

The main adjustment in the terms of reference related to 'spelling out' CBAC's responsibility at the national level of the Church; highlighting the responsibility of the Committee in respect of its support to black members of General Synod, as well as to the dioceses.

Part 3

Building credibility and developing overseas links

chapter 5
Seeds of Hope: Report of a Survey on Combating Racism in the Dioceses of the Church of England

Many Black Anglicans carry in their souls the suffering of rejection at the hands of their mother Church, the Church of England. Because of these past hurts, some still find it difficult to hear any news of newness … How can we demonstrate, especially to many young black people in this country, that the Church of England is still their spiritual home – yes, a home for all British people, and not just for Englishmen?[1]

Today the eradication of racism is a serious task for all of us. It is not some optional liberal gesture towards black people, because racism cannot co-exist with the Holy Spirit either in the human heart or in the Body of Christ. 'He who does not love his brother whom he has seen, cannot love God whom he has not seen' asserts Holy Scripture (1 John 4.20). Any 'security' or 'self-value' which racism appears to offer is false, and those who cradle it to their breast put their eternal destiny at risk. This survey is not a giant step, but it can be a tool. If the human will in the Church of England coincides with the divine will for the eradication of the sin of racism, it can prove a very useful tool. I trust many in the dioceses will find it so.[2]

Background

Shortly after I assumed duties in December 1987, Bishop Wilfred Wood, CBAC's Chairman held meetings with me in order to discuss my role and responsibilities. Bishop Wilfred identified the need for a survey to be done with the dioceses in order to determine the extent to which dioceses were/were not combating institutional racism. Bishop Wilfred felt that the questionnaire should be brief and he suggested some draft questions that were discussed by the committee.

The final questionnaire was incorporated in a letter addressed to the diocesan bishops, from the Committee's Chairman and is presented in the

Seeds of Hope report as an Appendix. The survey was undertaken by the Committee in 1988, in cooperation with the Board for Social Responsibility's Race and Community Relations Committee, chaired by the Revd Stanton Durant. The Committee received a 100 per cent response from the dioceses. The survey objectives were namely:

1. to gather information on racism in the dioceses and the work being done to combat it;

2. to identify good practice which might be shared with other dioceses;

3. to encourage dioceses to think theologically about racial justice issues;

4. to place racial justice issues on a higher level of priorities with respect to the Church's mission in the dioceses.[3]

Inadvertently the Diocese of Durham had not been sent the questionnaire. Bishop David Jenkins promptly phoned to say that he had heard about the survey and wondered why Durham was not included. This was quickly remedied and they returned the completed questionnaire. On more than one occasion after that Bishop David would drop into my office to say hello while attending the Synod.

The replies were revealing and ranged from dioceses like Southwark and Birmingham which had set up strategies for combating racism including the formulation of Equal Opportunities Policies, to dioceses which had no intention of doing anything as implied in their replies, e.g. Sheffield; as well as several rural dioceses which remarked there were no black people in their area and so there was no problem! Of course that myth was to be disabused when by 1994 the Committee, and the Statistical Department published the survey of 13,000 parishes which looked at black membership in the Church of England. *The survey showed that there were black Anglicans in every diocese.*

Interestingly since then, the Diocese of Sheffield has become one of the leading dioceses in several aspects of the work due to a very active group, led by persons such as Miss Cynthia Sutherland, and the Bishop's appointment of an Adviser in Black Anglican Concerns – Mrs Carmen Franklin. The diocese has debated *Seeds of Hope* and the *Passing Winter*, and Diocesan Synod approved an Equal Opportunities Policy. The Sheffield Black Anglican Concerns Group has conducted training on racial justice issues, in preparation for the annual Racial Justice Sunday and has been instrumental in planning regional meetings for black Anglicans. Bishop John Gladwin, who served there as Provost before his appointment as

Bishop of Guildford, assisted greatly in promoting the work in Sheffield
Diocese.

*Seeds of Hope: Report of a Survey on Combating Racism in the
Dioceses of the Church of England* was to be a seminal report in the
development of CBAC's work. Although the survey was carried out during
the existence of the first Committee, the final report was published,
launched at a press conference and debated in Autumn 1991, when the new
Committee was set up under the chairmanship of the Revd Canon Dr John
Sentamu. This decision was taken by the outgoing Committee in order to
ensure that the new Synod would have the opportunity to debate the report
as it would be an important item on their agenda, and also to ensure that
the new CBAC would own the report and ensure its follow-up, especially in
the dioceses.

Launch of the report – the press conference

The Revd Canon Dr John Sentamu, Chairman of the Committee on Black
Anglican Concerns (CBAC), the Revd Theo Samuel, Chairman of the Survey
Team and Mrs Glynne Gordon-Carter, Committee Secretary, launched the
Report at a press conference on Tuesday, 22 October 1991, facilitated by the
Director of Communications, the Revd Eric Shegog. The Conference was
very well attended, eventually there was only standing room! Coverage by
print as well as electronic media was good. There was a high level of interest
in the Report. In fact, the Communications Department recorded 69
enquiries including 16 interview requests. The Department was not able to
confirm the number of television and radio interviews which were held
locally as well as nationally. However, the Department felt that all requests
received were serious. Some newspaper captions read: 'The Church of
England is racist says new survey'; 'So just why are so many people racist?
Intolerance in Church'; 'The perils of meeting racists'; 'Synod backs action
to beat racism'; 'A report that Synod and the Church must take seriously'.
The Committee received several letters from members of the public. Most
were telling of their experience of racism and supporting the report. The
wide media coverage encouraged discussion and debate within the Church
at all levels, as well as the wider society. In the latter case, it appeared to be
the society looking in at the church and its attempts to 'grasp the nettle' of
racism. There was a flurry of activity and interest around the publication of
the Report. This was indeed a landmark in the life of the General Synod,
because for the first time the Church of England was having a debate on
racism within its structures and how to combat it.

The General Synod debate

The report was debated on Wednesday, 13 November 1991 in a two-hour, good-spirited and yet serious debate. The two motions that were put to the General Synod were carried overwhelmingly:

1. That this report be received.
2. That this Synod, affirming that all men and women of every hue and ethnic group belong to the one human race, are all made in the image of God and that each is of unique worth in His sight, commend the recommendations in Chapter 5 of the Report for discussion and action as appropriate by Boards and Councils of the General Synod, by dioceses, deaneries and parishes.

Only a handful voted against both motions.

The recommendations which were set out covered several issues, namely:

1. The diocese and its commitment to combating racism through its structures.
2. The role of the Diocesan Board of Education in combating racism.
3. The participation of black people in the life of the Church.
4. The Church as an employer – its commitment to equal opportunity.
5. Relationships with other black Christians.
6. Relationship with people of other faiths.
7. Racial justice issues within the wider society.

Included under item 1 were sections on support for white clergy, support for black clergy, training for clergy and the role of theological colleges. I will comment on these matters further in the report.

'Follow up' to the *Seeds of Hope* report

Perhaps these words from Bishop John Sentamu, in his introductory speech to the General Synod in support of the report, best summarizes how the Church should approach the work to be done:

> Its title *Seeds of Hope* is a clarion call for the Church of England to face its past, present and future vis à vis minority ethnic groups with courage born of the spirit of the crucified, risen and ascended Lord. We must resist at all cost, throughout this debate, the temptation of playing it safe and inviting others to do the changing. If we are to be reconcilers, we cannot remain neutral: for the Cross of Jesus shows us

how supremely costly is the work of reconciliation. This means developing a radical theology which takes into account the cultural and ethnic dimensions, as well as the political, social, economic and institutional structures.

Bishop John continued,

the Committee is very mindful of its role to support and resource dioceses in their task of combating racism. Thus every effort will be made to encourage and to build on good practices found in dioceses and to encourage some dioceses to learn from these good practices. The Committee on Black Anglican Concerns has set up an Advisory Group consisting of members of the Survey Team as well as other members of the Committee, because CBAC sees itself as having received a mandate from the Standing Committee and the General Synod's overwhelming support to follow up the Report. The follow up to *Seeds of Hope* will be demanding the full attention of the Committee.

Copies of *Seeds of Hope* were sent to Diocesan Secretaries, Suffragan Bishops, Secretaries of BSR and officers in dioceses with responsibility for race relations work. *The resolutions from the General Synod debate made it clear that follow up was expected at every level.*

The Chairman wrote and thanked the House of Bishops for their support and the time that they had given on the two occasions for him to address the Bishops about the report. In his letter he spoke about the follow up which was expected. *It was explained that a sequel to* Seeds of Hope *would be written within five years and which would set out progress that had been made by the dioceses.*

I felt that the success of the General Synod debate had given the CBAC the endorsement which it needed to progress its work. The *Caribbean Times* remarked, 'This is a brave effort to close the stable door after the horse has bolted'.

Since then the majority of the dioceses have debated *Seeds of Hope*. Also the report has been used as a resource by other denominations, and by research students. The *Seeds of Hope* Advisory Group which was chaired by Prebendary Theo Samuel concentrated mainly on the following areas: it monitored the work in dioceses especially related to diocesan motions in support of *Seeds of Hope,* worked with GS Boards and Councils, initiated the survey of black Anglicans, carried out several Advisory Team visits to dioceses, prepared *The Passing Winter*, a sequel to *Seeds of Hope* and the *Seeds of Hope in the Parish Study Pack.*

It is important to set the record straight on misinformation related to the *Seeds of Hope* publication. The title of the report was selected arising out of a conversation which I had with Bishop Wilfred during his time as Chairman in which he spoke of the report as a little 'seed of hope'. The cover was designed by Mrs Peggy Chapman from Wales. She was recommended to me by the Publications Unit. We had several telephone conversations about what the design should convey in keeping with the title and the nature of the report – hence the distinctive cover. Since then Mrs Chapman has done other designs for the Committee. Due to the demand, by 1994, *Seeds of Hope* had been reprinted for a third time – not too many church reports have that record!

Impact of *Seeds of Hope*

The significance of the *Seeds of Hope* report cannot be overstated. In my opinion it did the following:

1. For the first time ever the Church of England through the General Synod debated the existence of racism within its structures; and henceforth placed it firmly on the Church's agenda.
2. The survey helped to raise the level of awareness on 'race' issues in the dioceses.
3. The survey was able to identify good practice in the dioceses.
4. The survey helped the Committee to determine the level of assistance which the dioceses would require.
5. The survey helped to build the Committee's credibility in the Church.
6. The survey helped to bring the work to the attention of the entire Church and beyond.

chapter 6
Contact with the Church in North America

Shortly after my appointment, the Revd Canon Dr Harold Lewis, Staff Officer for Black Ministries at the Episcopal Church Centre in New York, wrote and introduced himself. Canon Lewis informed me that he had addressed the Archbishop's Commission on Urban Priority Areas in 1984 (the body which produced *Faith in the City*), re. the need to establish an office similar to his which would have as its primary focus a ministry on behalf of black communicants. He pledged the 'continued support of the office of Black Ministries and other agencies of the Episcopal Church as may be applicable in the establishment and development of Office for Black Affairs'. Canon Lewis' genuine support over the years meant that he became a colleague and trusted friend. He extended an invitation for me to visit and observe the work which was being done by the Episcopal Church, USA (ECUSA) in race relations. In those days I was very much the 'new girl on the block' as I was new to the job and to a great extent also new to British society – because whereas many people from the Caribbean could boast of having lived in England for 20 or 30 years, at the time I had just clocked up one year. We agreed that the visit should be postponed until 1989.

My visit to North America, which was planned for 4–30 June 1989, was approved by the Committee on Black Anglican Concerns as well as the BSR's Race and Community Relations Committee. Bishop John Gladwin (then Prebendary and Secretary to BSR) advised that the trip would be even more beneficial if it included a visit to the Anglican Church in Canada as well. Mrs Jeanne Rowles, Director of Social Action Ministries of the Anglican Church of Canada in Toronto, appointed two of her staff to arrange an itinerary, namely, the Revd Dr Laverne Jacobs, Co-ordinator, Council for Native Ministries and Mrs Irene Fraser, Consultant Human Rights Unit.

Objectives of the North American visit

1. To have the opportunity of getting an insight into the work being done with indigenous and minority communities by the Anglican Church in Canada through the work of the Co-ordinator for Native Ministries.

2. To experience at first hand the work being done by the Staff Officer for Black Ministries in the Episcopal Church.

3. To experience the Annual Conference of the Union of Black Episcopalians.

4. To inform the Church in North America of the work being done to combat racism at the national level of the Church of England.

5. To meet with representatives of secular organizations involved in community and race relations programmes.

My impressions

The visit to the Anglican Church in Canada, as well as ECUSA highlighted for me some challenges which they shared in common with the Church of England on minority issues, such as the need for more black clergy and black leadership, the employment issues which black clergy faced and the need for the Church to make room for black people. And yet there were differences. In Canada, Native issues had a higher profile than black and other minority issues. Native people did not wish to be pulled into the multi-cultural agenda. 'As first nation people their issues were distinct, they should not be diluted', stated Roland Kwano, Multi-Cultural Officer, United Church of Canada. Black Anglicans in Canada were not speaking out about issues which affected them although there was a lot of discontent with the structures of the Church. In some areas, despite the fact that there were a number of black worshippers, their issues did not get on parish, diocesan or national agendas. Toronto had many native clergy but few black clergy. In both Toronto and Montreal, young black people were inclined to leave the Anglican Church and join the black-led churches.

In Canada, where pressure to be involved in the structures of the Church came from Native people, black Anglicans appeared to be complacent and reluctant to question the Church. *In Montreal, the francophone element within the Church was seen as a huge task to be addressed as Anglicanism had no roots in French culture, consequently there were no liturgies, music, books or theology to appeal to immigrants for instance from the Haitian community.*

In ECUSA, under the leadership of Canon Harold Lewis and the Union of Black Episcopalians, black people were encouraged 'to become involved in the total life of the church on every level and in every way – mission, stewardship, evangelism, education, sharing, liberation, empowerment, leadership, governance and politics'. In 1988, black bishops, priests and deacons in ECUSA numbered 486. There were 19 black postulants and candidates for Holy Order. There were 23 black staff employed in senior positions in the Episcopal Church Centre – a large percentage of support staff were black. I was struck by the excellent attendance at church services where there were black worshippers.

> My visit to the church in Canada and the USA could be described in many ways as exciting, informative, enlightening, constructive, challenging and tiring. Days were long ending usually at 11.00 pm. On Sundays I addressed congregations, there were breakfast meetings, business luncheons and in between meetings over coffee – all in an effort to learn as much as possible. At times it was exhausting as my schedule entailed travelling several hundred, and sometimes thousands, of miles. Despite a very heavy schedule there were pleasant interludes which helped me to unwind and recharge mentally and physically for the next day's events.[1]

My report was deliberately detailed in parts as I tried to provide useful insights on the work in race issues in Canada and the USA, the views of minority people in the Church, as well as glimpses of the work which was being done by secular agencies.

The report included eleven recommendations, nine of which referred specifically to the work which should be done by the Church of England in combating racism, with the help of CBAC. It is very encouraging that most of the nine have been tackled.

Following on from the visit to ECUSA, the Episcopal Commission for Black Ministries endorsed Canon Lewis' suggestion that two young people from the Church of England should be invited to the Conference of the Black Episcopalians (25–29 June 1991) in Philadelphia. CBAC selected Miss Sarah Adelaja and Mr Leon Hasler to attend the Conference. They were accompanied by the Revd Charles Lawrence, a member of CBAC. The cost of their airline tickets was paid by the Episcopal Commission for Black Ministries. Money to cover accommodation costs was raised by CBAC on presentation of a project proposal to both Archbishops, various dioceses and other church agencies. The generous response from dioceses resulted in a surplus which contributors agreed should be retained and used for the Youth exchange visit from the USA planned for 1993.

Other involvement with the Episcopal Church

1. In April 1988, I gave a brief presentation to the Pre-Lambeth Afro-Anglican Bishops' Symposium held at Cambridge and organized by Canon Lewis.

2. Canon Lewis attended and addressed CBAC's 1994 Black Anglican Celebration for the Decade of Evangelism held at the University of York.

3. I was invited to serve as a member of the International Planning Group which organized the Afro-Anglicanism Conference on Identity, Integrity, Impact which was held at the University of the Western Cape, in South Africa under the patronage of Archbishop Desmond Tutu, in 1995.

4. I delivered an address at the 1998 Pre-Lambeth Afro-Anglican Bishop's Symposium held at Newnham College, Cambridge University which was also organized by Canon Lewis.

5. A group of Young African-American Episcopalians from the Society of Absalom Jones, Howard University, Washington, led by the Revd Dr Carleton Hayden, Chaplain and Tutor, came on a pilgrimage in May 2001. CMEAC was responsible for arranging their itinerary and accommodation for the two-week visit. Mr Rob McSwain, Research Fellow at Lambeth Palace, greatly assisted with planning the itinerary. Absalom Jones was the first black man to be ordained a priest in ECUSA.

The Revd Lynne Collins, Canon Lewis' successor, invited me to visit ECUSA in 1998. The itinerary was very interesting and included visits to the Church Centre in New York, Detroit, Los Angeles and Philadelphia. In Los Angeles I was struck by the work which a parish priest was doing in his parish. He was working part-time with the Church yet he was ministering to English-speaking as well as Spanish-speaking congregations. The Spanish-speaking service on a Sunday morning was 'packed out'. The priest informed me (fifteen minutes before the service) that he wanted me to address that congregation. I explained to him that I did not speak Spanish ('O' Level Spanish long forgotten!). He said that was not a problem as he would translate. He suggested that I should robe because I would need to sit in the sanctuary as the church was usually full. What an experience! Whole families were at worship – including grandparents and whereas the first service was in English, the liturgy and hymns for the second service were in Spanish. This was truly a community worshipping together.

It was clear that church growth in Los Angeles was mainly among the Hispanics. I was told that the attendance at the Episcopal Church surpassed another denomination nearby; without a doubt this was due to the response of the parish priest to the needs of an ethnic group, the Hispanic community. They had found a spiritual home, and one in which they were comfortable.

The Revd Lynne Collins, Officer for Black Ministries ECUSA, was due to pay a return visit. Her itineray would have included attendance at some of the General Synod 1998 July sessions. Unfortunately she had to cancel that visit due to restructuring at the Episcopal Church Centre.

Since the visit to the Anglican Church in Canada, the Revd Laverne Jacobs and his wife visited England at the invitation of one of the missionary societies. The Committee hosted a luncheon in their honour at which they met Committee members, as well as ecumenical partners. I have been informed that black Anglicans in Toronto have started to come together and they hold a service of thanksgiving each year at St Paul's Church in Toronto.

Invitation from the Church of Scotland (1990)

An invitation was extended by the Revd Steven Mackie to visit Scotland and meet with the Working Party on Racism, a group which had been set up by the Church of Scotland in conjunction with other churches. The purpose of the visit was to familiarize the Scottish group with the Church of England's programme, as well as to be advised of some of the issues in Scotland and how the churches were trying to respond.

They arranged a four-day itinerary which included meetings with representative of the Scottish Episcopal Church. A luncheon was hosted by the Scottish Episcopal Church which was attended by bishops, the Mission Board Convenors, as well as several members of staff at the offices of the General Synod. This provided an opportunity for sharing with the group the work which was being done at the national, as well as diocesan, levels of the Church of England. Invitees were particularly interested in the survey which was being carried out on instruments for combating racism in the dioceses.

chapter 7

Reflections on the early years

In 1987, when I was appointed to the post as Secretary to BSR's Race and Community Relations Committee and seconded to work with the Committee on Black Anglican Concerns, that was a real challenge.

I was relatively new to the society and certainly new to the structures of the Church of England. This meant I had to learn as quickly as possible about both situations. During my first year, I travelled around a great deal in order to meet with people in the dioceses, including Diocesan Bishops, persons in other denominations who had been doing race relations work, and also persons in secular agencies. The idea was to immerse myself fully in the work so that I could understand the issues and be in a position to advise both committees.

For the first time the Church of England was being challenged to combat institutional racism, the CBAC was breaking new ground. Therefore it was a matter of educating the Church to understand the nature of racism, the fact that it disadvantages people and more so to understand that the Church itself through its institutions might be unwittingly acting in a racist manner. This was going to be an uphill task! We often got comments like 'How could the church be racist? After all we are Christians.'

Bishop Wilfred Wood in his capacity as Chairman of CBAC was extremely supportive. He held regular meetings with me, offered very helpful advice on how to proceed and informed me about the history of black people's struggle in British society (often from his own experiences). This made me want to learn more and so by 1990 I registered for the MSc. in Race and Ethnic Relations at Birkbeck College, London University, which I completed by 1992.

The CBAC members were fully involved in the work and never saw it as a situation where they just attended Committee meetings. Additionally each member was involved in an area of the Committee's work in which they had an interest. It was clear that for some members, especially those representing GS Boards and Councils they had a lot to learn about the issues in order to understand what the Committee wanted to achieve. Some became the strongest advocates and would speak openly on the floor of GS about their 'conversion' experience. Archdeacon David Silk who became Bishop of Ballarat in Australia was one such person. There was camaraderie in Committee meetings yet a great deal was achieved because members were dedicated and focused about the work, despite the odds, such as lack of adequate resources.

The Race and Community Relations Committee's (RCRC) brief was concerned with wider racial justice issues, as against CBAC's responsibility which was working within the structures to combat institutional racism. The RCRC was interesting in its membership because members included persons from other denominations so there was a broader view and the Committee was involved in issues such as discrimination against black people in employment, housing, black people in prisons and education and immigration. On two occasions, the Revd Stanton Durant, Chairman, and the Secretary were members of BSR delegation which went to the Home Secretary to discuss immigration matters. During my early years in Church House, Prebendary John Gladwin (now Bishop of Guildford), who was then Secretary to BSR, was very committed to the work and was not just paying lip service to it. I felt well supported by him and, he ensured that I was given proper office accommodation. My predecessor, the Revd Ken Leech, had described his office as 'one of the smallest rooms in Church House'. I was given staff support – a personal secretary, and was made to feel a part of the BSR team. During my first week, while settling in, BSR's Secretary advised me that I should remember to take my days in lieu because the Church was a hard taskmaster.

Very early in my time at Church House, Mr Deryck Pattinson, Secretary General, requested a meeting during which he made it clear that he was fully supportive of the work and I should not hesitate in approaching him if his assistance was required. So I was fortunate in the moral support, advice and assistance which both Committees provided, as well as colleagues in Church House. Messrs Nigel Barnett and Andrew Nunn assisted the Committee on administrative matters related to the General Synod.

Before I started to write this report, during an interview with Bishop John Gladwin, he reflected on the work during those early years. Bishop John stated that in 1985 the publication of *Faith in City* changed the debate. It raised questions about General Synod and the Church of England and, in particular, what were they going to do about the implicit racism? The General Synod board secretaries, of their own volition and with the encouragement of Mr Pattinson (the Secretary General), were committed to doing something about minority ethnic issues across the organization. This led to them pressing for change, and that began with my appointment. Bishop Gladwin said that when I was released to work for CBAC, the agenda on 'race' was not just a social responsibility issue any longer. My transfer to work full-time for CBAC was the point of transition to the General Synod; the CBAC was taking on the responsibility for the General Synod agenda on that issue.

In 1990, when the decision was taken to have me concentrate full-time on CBAC's work, I felt that was a great pity because despite distinctive agendas the committees' work was interrelated. In my opinion, a better decision would have been to recruit an assistant to work with me to serve both Committees. The RCRC's work never really thrived after that; members felt demoralized because in their eyes the Committee's work was downgraded as the officer had been reassigned. Members also felt that BSR had not consulted them properly. In fact as stated earlier in the report, the Revd Stanton Durant, RCRC's Chairman resigned in protest.

In the *Church Times* of the 28 March 1991, the Revd Ken Leech and Miss Mavis Fernandes (his secretary while in post), wrote an article 'A topic that will not disappear' in which he commented on BSR and the limiting of its work on race.

> The recent removal of Mrs Glynne Gordon-Carter to work entirely with the Committee on Black Anglican Concerns is the culmination of the process well known in the secular bureaucracies as 'rationalisation', a familiar euphemism for back tracking ... After all the struggles to get racial justice on the agenda of the central structures, this is where we have got to. A committee established only after years of struggle, loses its full-time worker within the first few years of its existence.

Within the space of just three years, between 1987 and 1990, both CBAC and RCRC had faced crises. In the case of CBAC the failure of the GS debate in February 1989 strengthened the Committee in terms of support, especially from the Diocesan Bishops and the dioceses. With respect to the RCRC the thrust of their work was weakened and never regained its momentum.

Part 4
Affirming black Anglicans 1991–2001

The 1994 Black Anglican Celebration for the Decade of Evangelism (22–24 July 1994, University of York)

This section of the report will identify strategies which were implemented by the Committee to affirm, value and celebrate the gifts of black Anglicans.

> The exercise of power is a complex subject full of pitfalls. It is however, one that must be addressed if we are to be true to our Master. One gift which Black Anglicans may offer to God's Church is to help us towards a better understanding of the true nature and right use of power. This will become clearer as more black people take up positions of responsibility in the structures of the church.[1]

> The first need is to be alive, to be joyful, to point to the fact that there is something more to life than secular reality, by the fact that we are ourselves enjoying that something more. My prayer for Black Anglicans is that you may inject some of your aliveness and joyfulness in the whole body of the Church. It is one of the gifts you bring – and don't be put off if it is not at first welcomed.[2]

> Churches with growing congregations are often driven by black people's exuberance in prayer and worship and their natural instinct for evangelism. I am sure that evangelism is one of the greatest gifts we have to give to the Church.[3]

Background

The chairmanship of the Committee under Bishop Wilfred Wood will be remembered mainly for the work which it did to lay the foundation, and begin the process of building the Committee's credibility in the Church of England; the determination of the Committee to 'grasp the nettle' in order to raise the Church's awareness of 'race' issues, and to support the Church in its task of combating institutional racism. The *Seeds of Hope* report and its recommendations laid down the agenda for the Church; also the discussions which the Committee had with chairmen and secretaries of the General Synod's Boards and Councils laid the foundation for future collaboration with them. As first Chairman, Bishop Wilfred had a difficult and unpopular task which he did not shirk. In the *Seeds of Hope* debate, Canon Sentamu (now Bishop of Stepney) remarked to the GS, 'the Bishop of Croydon's Foreword to *Seeds of Hope*, sets the report in a necessary historical context and out of that context challenges us all to the eradication of racism'.

The first Committee was responsible for seeking the approval of the GS Standing Committee to hold an event to affirm black Anglicans, as well as the initial planning of the 1994 Black Anglican Celebration for the Decade of Evangelism.

The discussions which led to the idea of the celebration were prompted by my report on the visit to the Anglican Church in Canada. They had held their first Native Anglican Convocation in 1988, organized by the Revd Laverne Jacobs, Co-ordinator, Council for Native Ministries. The point of the conference was first and foremost to bring Native Canadian Anglicans from the grassroots together for the first time in a large gathering, and to have them get to know one another, celebrate their common faith and identity, and name common concerns. The Convocation which brought together 180 Native Canadian Anglicans was a powerful affirming experience. Delegates included people of different dialects, lifestyles, level of contact with white society, political and social structures. There were elders among them who had no formal schooling and spoke no English. There were professionals who had studied and worked in Toronto and Montreal. There were people who had been involved for years in complicated legalistic land claims negotiations with federal bureaucrats and lawyers, and there were those who still lived by fishing and trapping.

The title of the Convocation report *Recovering the Feather* came from a dream which was recounted by Rose Evans of Norway House, Manitoba, who spoke for the first and only time during the week's events.

> As I was walking, I saw this beautiful big feather coming from the sky. And I didn't want it to touch the ground. I was going to catch it. Then all of a sudden it was pulled up.

> Then I heard voices laughing, and I looked up. It was the white people. They were controlling this feather; I could see the strings. And my

people were trying to get the feather. They were crying. But they were being controlled by the white society. And whatever the white men wanted it happened. Because they have this feather.

The Revd Jacobs introduced his work by showing me the video of the Convocation which left an indelible impression on me. Consequently, my first recommendation in the report of my visit to North America stated: 'A consultation should be held by black Anglicans in order to discuss issues of common concern and how best to develop and encourage their leadership potential at all levels of church life.'

Another event which confirmed my view that CBAC should host a big event to affirm black Anglicans was the Congress of Black Catholics held in London in 1990. I felt privileged to have been invited. I was inspired by this event *which affirmed black Catholics and encouraged them over a weekend to channel their enthusiasm, talents and desire to be full participants in the life of the Catholic Church in Britain.*

> We the Black Catholics in Britain want to tell our story – all the different stories of how Christ has met his many peoples and how he has lived with us as family. We want to tell our stories so as to rejoice in the salvation and identity he has given.[4]

My report on the Black Catholics Congress also started CBAC thinking about the possibility of planning an event for black Anglicans. After a great deal of discussion, members decided that a conference would be held. It was important that dates should be acceptable to the Archbishops of Canterbury and York as their attendance would be vital. The Revd Rajinder Daniel, member of CBAC, was asked to chair the Celebration Planning Group. With the succession of the new Committee under the chairmanship of Bishop John Sentamu, the planning of the event continued.

In discussing what the event should be called, a celebration was suggested as against a convocation as the latter might give too formal an impression. I remember one committee member posed the question, What is there to celebrate? The answer came back from various members of the Committee – the fact that black Anglicans are members of the Church of England and the importance of affirming and celebrating the gifts which they bring to the Church; and so the 1994 Black Anglican Celebration for the Decade of Evangelism was born. The Revd Daniel was not a member of the new committee, but it was decided that he should continue to chair the Planning Group and he was written to to that effect. The event had been originally planned for 1993 but the new committee felt that 1994 would be more appropriate as it would provide a longer time for planning a well-organized event.

The Committee felt that with the publication and GS debate of the *Seeds of Hope* report in 1991, it would be critical to bring together people from dioceses, parishes and the central structures in order to review, share and learn of good practice in parishes, deaneries and dioceses based on their response to *Seeds of Hope*.

Celebration objectives

1. To recognize, celebrate and rejoice in the diversity of gifts which black Anglicans bring to the Church.

2. To devise ways and means of encouraging young black Anglicans to remain and become involved in the Church at all levels.

3. To plan strategies towards using the gifts of black Anglicans in the task of evangelism.

4. To help black Anglicans develop confidence and leadership potential, and to offer this confidence as a gift to the whole Church.

5. To discuss the progress of dioceses towards implementing recommendations from *Seeds of Hope*.

6. To encourage the Church to live the Christian faith authentically and therefore to confront the society in areas of racial injustices. 'Evangelism and caring go hand in hand, the gospel needs demonstrating as well as proclaiming.'[5]

The pre-Celebration pack

The Celebration Planning Group decided that it was important to publish and launch an informative, professional and attractively presented pack in preparation for the event. The pack was launched at a press conference one year in advance in order to stir up interest at all levels of the Church and to encourage preparation at the parish levels – through discussion of the issues raised in the pack. The pack posed key questions and gave answers on Why the Celebration? What was it for? When and where would it be held? and Who would be involved? Guidance was given on how to use the pack in preparation for the event, prayers and Bible passages, issues in the Church, issues in the society, information on BSR's race relations work, CBAC's work with the structures, and ecumenical involvement through the support of the British Council of Church's Community Race Relations Unit. The pack also included a section on the definitions of words which we use when discussing 'race' issues, as well as useful resources. The Group responsible for writing the pack included some members of the CBAC as well as staff persons from the Board of Education and the Board of Mission and Unity, Mrs Hilary Ineson and Mrs Marion Mort respectively.

The pre-Celebration pack was central to the planning process in that it conveyed a sense of purpose to participants and assisted them in their preparations so that they came prepared to participate in what would be a significant event – for the first time ever black Anglicans were coming together in a national event. A few days before the event, one diocesan bishop telephoned me to say that he had not planned to attend but had received a copy of the pack and having read it he wanted to be there!

The celebration was held mainly for black Anglicans. Some came as representatives from dioceses, e.g. CBAC Diocesan Link Persons, others came as representatives from parishes and as individuals. There were representatives from all the dioceses including the Diocese of Europe which sent delegates from Belgium, Germany and Sweden. The Archbishops of Canterbury and York and over 30 bishops attended the event, as well as chairmen and secretaries of GS boards and councils. Their role was stated in the pack – they were to be involved as listeners, as participants in dialogue, and also in effective solidarity, decision-making and action. Observers from other churches, as well as church-based organizations attended. The Dioceses of Durham, Sodor and Man and Winchester sponsored between them three delegates from London and Southwark dioceses. The Lord Pitt Foundation provided sponsorship for one young delegate. This was arranged by Dame Jocelyn Barrow. GS boards and councils and the GS Standing Committee were well-represented. There were participants from the Association of Black Clergy, the Black Majority Churches, ecumenical observers and Anglican agencies such as the Mothers' Union, the United Society for the Propagation of the Gospel and the Church Missionary Society. A full list of participants is provided in Appendix B of *Roots and Wings*, the Celebration report.

A great deal of effort was put into planning every aspect of the Celebration – several people were involved in the various groups which 'fed' information to the Celebration Planning Group, and then to CBAC for approval and implementation. The Committee also consulted with the wider network – Diocesan Link Persons (DLPs). With the help of the diocesan bishop and the DLPs, the dioceses nominated young black Anglicans to attend a meeting hosted by CBAC in Church House. This was held on Saturday, 28 November 1992, when the Committee brought together for the first time a group of young people from the dioceses to consult with them on their views about the forthcoming event.

They made it clear that they should not be invited to be just stewards as they wanted to be truly involved in the Celebration. CBAC asked diocesan bishops to ensure that young people were included in diocesan delegations. The Committee targeted and sponsored the attendance of 30 young persons from the following dioceses: Birmingham, Chelmsford, Leicester, Lichfield, Liverpool, London, Manchester, Peterborough, Sheffield, Southwark and St Albans. The 17 workshop facilitators were assisted by young people who acted as co-facilitators. In the end over 70 participants who attended the Celebration were under 35 years of age. In the final Plenary Session two of them were invited to reflect on the Celebration.

A success

Many referred to the Celebration as a watershed, a success, a significant event in the life of the Church of England, a renewal of hope, an indication

Figure 1: Participants at the Black Anglican Celebration, University of York, July 1994.

of what the Church should be, a shared vision, an enriching and powerful experience.

It was indeed a watershed because for the first time in the life of the Church of England, Archbishops, Bishops and other key people in the church were meeting with black Anglicans to discuss, share, pray, worship, laugh, play and eat together over a weekend residential conference. It was a watershed experience because for the first time black Anglicans were coming together from all over England and from different persuasions to be seen, heard, listened to and affirmed in their ministries as laity and clergy.[6]

The overwhelming success of the Celebration resounded for many months throughout the Church – dioceses, deaneries and parishes, and in fact the wider ecumenical scene as there were ecumenical observers present. In his reflections on the event, The Very Revd Robert Jeffery, Dean of Worcester, stated 'the conference was impressive, not only in representation from 42 dioceses (including Bishops) but a conference which was organised with graciousness and without rancour. It was the relaxed style and the good humour of the conference which struck me most' (*Roots and Wings*). The Committee tried to encapsulate all of these experiences in the video, and in *Roots and Wings*, the report of the celebration (the title of which came from the Celebration hymn composed by the Revd Canon Patrick Rushevel); so that for the nearly 400 participants they would act as reminders of that eventful weekend, and for others they would get some understanding of the event. *The Trumpet Call*, the final statement from the 17 workshops which addressed the Church of England and its leaders, English society and ourselves and our God, is recorded in *Roots and Wings* and *The Passing Winter* reports.

There were many good things about the Celebration. The involvement of younger delegates, their dynamism, their confidence and the contributions which they brought were outstanding. Bishop Colin Buchanan in his reflections stated 'I was also very struck by the relative youthfulness of so many of our black participants. They were giving us the truth the way it is, and generally without hesitation' (*Roots and Wings*). Captain Rayman Khan as a young black person spoke passionately in his reflections about the need for young people to be empowered and encouraged to participate in the life of the Church:

We need to take risks alongside them, to give them space to explore and experience the faith in ways that are relevant and interesting to them. I await the day when our young people, with their idealism, energy, commitment and faith can challenge and enrich our church, for we are poor without them.[7]

Figure 2: Dr Protasia Torkington addressing the Black Anglican Celebration. Canon Smith-Cameron, Celebration Chaplain, is on the right.

There were key-note speeches by both archbishops; Mr Herman Ouseley (now Lord Ouseley) who was the Chairman of the Commission for Racial Equality; Dr Protasia Torkington, member of the Roman Catholic Church; the Revd Canon Dr Cyril Ockorocha, Officer for the Decade of Evangelism of the Anglican Communion; Miss Josile Munro, member of GS; the Revd Charles Lawrence, member of CBAC; the Revd Rajinder Daniel, Chairman Celebration Planning Group and the Revd Canon Dr John Sentamu, Chairman of CBAC. These set the scene for a most inspiring weekend. The Celebration received very wide coverage from the print and electronic media, both nationally and locally, prior to, during and after the event. *The Revd Eric Shegog, Director of Communications, informed us that all told the Celebration had received the widest coverage of any Church of England event within recent years.*

The Celebration left an indelible impression on participants. I have included here some comments from evaluation sheets, and many letters and cards which the Committee received:

- many thanks for an unforgettable experience;

- the meticulous planning was evident but did not constrain the Celebration which indeed it was;
- with the Celebration, the Church of England took a great step without precedent in its history;
- variety and range of workshops – excellent;
- no one accused me of being racist but the discussions and conversations forced me to consider whether I was in fact racist;
- a very happy and refreshing time;
- the pre-Celebration pack was remarkable;
- it was a good experience, so much breadth and we certainly went home on a high which even (in my case) sustained me through four hours driving through torrential rain and thunderstorm. A very good weekend and a privilege for me to be able to share it with you.

The Central Board of Finance (CBF) was prepared to underwrite the Celebration. The Central Church Fund provided financial assistance for the production of the pre-Celebration pack and the conference report. The Archbishop of York financed the video which was produced by Mr Frank Harris. It should be noted that to CBAC's credit the conference expenses came in below the budget! The Chairman of the CBF complimented the committee on its control of the Celebration expenses at a CBAC meeting which he attended a few years later.

At the closing act of worship an offering of £739.00 was collected towards the Rwanda Appeal.

Figure 3: The crèche at the Black Anglican Celebration, University of York, July 1994.

Post-Celebration

Where do we go from here and how best can the results of the Celebration be incorporated into the lifeblood of the Church? This was the concern of the Secretary General and also of the Committee, a number of strategies were implemented accordingly:

i) The House of Bishops

The Chairman of CBAC addressed the House of Bishops at its meeting in January on the multi-faceted recommendations from the Celebration in *Roots and Wings*.

ii) Local level

- The Celebration report was sent to all participants.

- The Committee wrote to all delegates from parishes, regarding their role in the follow up to the Celebration.

- Dioceses, deaneries and parishes were being encouraged to purchase copies of the report and video as they were very useful training aids.

- In some dioceses, Bishops held debriefing meetings with their delegates in an effort to explore ways in which their dioceses could respond to the issues which had been raised by the Celebration. In other dioceses, delegates were invited to present reports to diocesan synods, deanery synods, PCCs and parishes. The encouragement given by Diocesan Bishops led to some dioceses holding their own celebration events; some delegates gave media interviews, and wrote articles on the event in diocesan magazines. The Committee was particularly pleased that in some dioceses Bishops had written their reflections on the Celebration in the diocesan newspaper/leaflet, as many of them had come with their diocese. In 1995, the Committee in Liverpool held a regional conference which was attended by participants from Chester, London, Liverpool, Manchester, Sheffield, Southwell, and Wakefield dioceses.

   Inspired by the Celebration, dioceses which previously had not taken up the challenge in *Seeds of Hope* have since discussed appropriate plans of action.[8]

iii) General Synod boards and councils

Representatives of GS boards and councils were written to with respect to their role in following up the Celebration.

iv) General Synod

The Chairman gave a report on the Celebration to the Policy and Standing Committees. He wrote to both archbishops to request their permission for a presentation to be made at the GS November sessions:

> this was such a momentous occasion and I am writing therefore to ask whether it is at all possible at the next Group of Sessions for the General Synod, for a presentation to be made at the beginning of the Synod. I think the Synod needs to hear good news ...

CBAC was asked to lead the worship and report to the Synod the experience of the Celebration on the second day of the November Group of Sessions. The presentation on the Celebration was organized by Canon Smith-Cameron, Celebration Chaplain, and took the form of worship. The Revd Gilbert Lee, Mrs Nell Hall-Wycherley, Miss Rebecca Selvarajasingham and Mr Richard Bobb participated through their contributions of dance, music and song. Testimonies were given by the Most Revd and Rt Hon. John Habgood, the Archbishop of York, Mrs Penny Granger, Ms Smitha Prasadam, Mrs Ayodele Gansallo, and Mr David Dean; the last three mentioned were young participants from St Albans and Manchester dioceses. Archbishop Habgood described his response to the Indian classical dance in the worship at York Minster as a 'converting experience'.

Minority ethnic Anglicans

For minority ethnic Anglicans, the Celebration was a time of affirmation, a time of gathering new strength, confidence and new hope. Thereafter some committed themselves to exploring vocations within the Church and have since been ordained. One person said that for him the deciding moment came when he attended the

Figure 4: Indian classical dance formed part of the worship at York Minister during the Black Anglican Celebration. The dancer is Miss Rebecca Selvarajasingham.

service at York Minster and heard Bishop Wilfred Wood's sermon (first Chairman of CBAC). A number of people went on to be trained as Readers, others have become much more involved in their local church; some have been elected to serve on diocesan boards/ or councils and in some instances subsequently became members of General Synod.

As someone who was very involved in the planning of the Celebration from its inception in 1990 and saw it through all its stages, for me it was an immense joy to see the event come to fruition – with the arrival of all participants, the expectancy which was in the air, the feeling of togetherness which existed throughout the weekend, the fellowship, the discussions, the genuine involvement and contribution of participants, and the culmination of the Celebration in *The Trumpet Call*.

My one regret was hearing afterwards that there were white clergy, as well as some black clergy, who had kept the information about the Celebration away from their black parishioners as they did not want them to attend. Hopefully some would have read about the event through the *Church Times*, the *Church of England Newspaper*, *The Independent*, *The Telegraph*, the Catholic *Tablet* and the *Yorkshire Post*.

CBAC's response to the Celebration

The Chairman and members of CBAC were extremely pleased about the success of the Celebration. It had been a watershed event in the mission and ministry of the Church of England.

The Celebration was not only a rallying of the dioceses with respect to the needs of black Anglicans, it was also a rallying of the Committee to those needs and so the following action areas were agreed:

1. the setting up of the Celebration Implementation Group;
2. the redesignation of CBAC;
3. the review of the Committee's Terms of Reference;
4. the setting up of the Liturgy Sub-Committee.

1. The Celebration Implementation Group (CIG)

The main role of the CIG was to monitor the follow-up work to the Celebration in GS boards and councils, and the dioceses. The Group monitored the response of GS boards and councils, as well as the response form the dioceses for approximately one year and then was disbanded.

2. The redesignation of the Committee

The decision to change the Committee's name from the Committee on Black Anglican Concerns to the Committee for Minority Ethnic Anglican Concerns (CMEAC) in 1995 was not taken lightly. Members felt that the change of name would enable the Committee to be more inclusive of all minority ethnic Anglicans.

> But why the redesignation? Arising out of the Celebration and the issues which were raised CBAC took the views that the title 'minority ethnic' would be more inclusive as some people who experienced discrimination on grounds of colour, culture and ethnic background had found it difficult to identify with the term 'black'. After a great deal of discussion, members decided on 'minority ethnic' as a more inclusive term which would encompass African, African-Caribbean, Asian, Black British, Chinese and many others who felt that they were still being marginalised by the church on grounds of colour, culture and ethnic origins. This means also that what people traditionally referred to as white would be appropriate to refer to as majority ethnic.[9]

3. The review of the Committee's Terms of Reference

The Committee's Terms of Reference had been revised in 1990. By 1995, in order to respond better to the needs of minority ethnic Anglicans, the committee decided to review its Terms of Reference. This would require CMEAC to take seriously the whole question of vocations, theology, liturgy and worship. By the end of 1995, the General Synods' Standing Committee gave tacit agreement to the Committee's proposal, i.e. its revised Terms of Reference, Constitution and redesignation. In January 1996, the new Standing Committee gave its approval. The revised Terms of Reference have been included in this report as Appendix 7, and the list of 1995 committee members is supplied as Appendix 8.

4. The Liturgy Sub-Committee

The Most Revd and Rt Hon. George Carey, Archbishop of Canterbury, in his key-note address at the Celebration had particularly highlighted worship and the diverse forms of spirituality centred in music which black Anglicans have to offer:

> I believe it is a dimension that will not only enrich our worship and liturgical life but will also add something exciting to our evangelism. I urge you to develop it and if you do, I can promise you my enthusiastic support.[10]

CMEAC held a one-day Consultation, the objectives of which were as follows:

- to explore ways and means of galvanizing and bringing together our rich diversity of gifts – music, poetry, art, drama, dance – the arts as an offering to the Church;

- to explore how to release people to glorify God within the structures;

- to explore how to make a contribution to discussion on liturgies in the Church of England, as all liturgies were going to be revised in the year 2000.

Interested people including liturgists were invited to the consultation and the discussions which were fruitful recognized strategies that would enrich the liturgy. In fact, that event helped the Committee to set up a Liturgy Sub-Committee under the chairmanship of the Revd George Kovoor in 1997. The Rt Revd David Stancliffe, Chairman of the Liturgical Commission, met with the Revd Kovoor so that the Commission could be made aware of the work that was being done.

The Liturgy Sub-Committee's agenda included the discussion of various liturgies, styles of worship and customs. This was exciting and interesting work that had the potential for further development. However the lack of staff resources to focus on this area of work as well as the busy schedules of members resulted in the work going into abeyance.

'*Common Worship*, is marked by diversity, not only in its content and in those who will use it ...'[11] However, many minority ethnic Anglicans have not considered the 2000 revised liturgy as good news as it has not incorporated or reflected the ethnic and cultural diversity of the Church of England. In my opinion the revision of the liturgy was a missed opportunity as the Church of England still has not embraced the distinctive styles of worship which black and Asian Christians bring as part of the shared styles of worship in the Church of England. This attitude is also reminiscent of the fact that the Church still continues to turn a deaf ear to the Committee's request for the need to have liturgies in Asian languages.

> Her Asian, African, Caribbean and other children offer through song, prayer, dance and music their own singular gifts of spirituality ... for the future of the Church of England all our spiritualities must find a resting place and together nourish the lives of the faithful...[12]

> ... the area that still needs to see a lot of unfreezing: the whole question of liturgy, highlighted in the report. Minority ethnic Anglican groups have much to offer to the Church from their insights and

experience in liturgy and spirituality – in music, in poetry, in dance and in drama –we need to find ways of maximising their distinctive and richly varied gifts during the next few years of liturgical change and development in the Church.[13]

I have spent a great deal of time reporting on the 1994 Black Anglican Celebration for the Decade of Evangelism because this was a watershed event and the tide really began to turn with the Celebration, since for the first time ever black Anglicans were being listened to by the structures.

How We Stand: A Report on Black Anglican Membership of the Church of England in the 1990s

The survey has been designed to reflect the main priorities for the Church stated by the General Synod's Standing Committee and endorsed by the Archbishops of Canterbury and York: the need to build up confidence, encourage evangelism and deepen the Church's unity ...[1]

We make no specific recommendations about changes in diocesan structures. But we consider that each diocese should review its organisational arrangements and the composition of its Boards, Councils and Committees to ensure that black Anglicans have a voice in decision making or advisory processes and that a concern for racial discrimination and disadvantage is reflected in all its policies.[2]

We cannot afford to rest either as a Church or as a Society until we have confronted racism at its deepest level – in our nation, in the structures of our Church, in the ordained ministry, in congregation life. Without each other we are less of the people God intends us to be.[3]

This survey was carried out between 1992–1993, completed by 1994, and launched at a press conference on 4 July 1994 a few days before the 1994 Black Anglican Celebration was held. The timing for the launch of the report was critical as the Committee felt that they would gather even more support for the Celebration, and in fact that had the desired effect. The main objective of the survey was to ascertain the number of black Anglicans in the Church and the extent of their participation in the life of the Church of England, throughout the 13,000 parishes.

In Church House there was a great deal of goodwill and support for the survey by the GS Standing Committee which approved the draft questionnaire. The House of Bishops, which reviewed the questionnaire, requested that a question should be included on other places of worship in the parish (Archbishop Habgood) and gave the survey their blessing. The Statistics Unit of the Central Board of Finance conducted the survey.

A great deal of time was spent in discussion with the Statistics Department so as to ensure that the questionnaire was clear and brief, yet hopefully it would encourage replies and yield very useful information from the parishes. We were sensitive to the fact that clergy receive a great deal of mail requesting information, so although it would be essential to get a good response the Committee did not want the clergy to feel burdened. Much was done to 'prepare the ground so that we would receive a good harvest'. The diocesan secretaries would be responsible for ensuring the circulation of the questionnaires so that the whole exercise was explained to them and their support solicited. This was on the advice of the Statistics Unit. A separate form was sent to cathedrals and the questionnaires were distributed with the CBF parochial returns. Mr Douglas Fryer (now deceased) who was the Head of Statistics, advised the Committee. Mr Raymond Tongue (deputy) conducted the analysis and wrote the report entitled *How We Stand*, based on the findings; CBAC was consulted at every stage.

Diocesan bishops supported the survey and some bishops wrote articles in their diocesan newsletters commending the questionnaires to the parishes. Many incumbents took the time to respond, in fact 60 per cent of the parishes returned the completed questionnaires. The Statistics Unit informed the Committee that the response was good and certainly beyond the returns that they usually received. The Unit received over a 70 per cent response rate from the following dioceses: Birmingham (74%), Blackburn (79%), Bradford (83%), Derby (71%), Durham (73%), Leicester (80%), Lichfield (96%), Liverpool (98%), Manchester (75%), Newcastle (86%), Portsmouth (74%), Ripon (73%), Southwark (79%), Worcester (80%) and York (72%). The report *How We Stand* created an awareness of the issues at the parish level and the survey helped the dioceses to locate parishes with black Anglicans.

In the report, black Anglicans are defined as those of Caribbean, African and Asian backgrounds. The survey indicated that there are 27,000 black Anglicans in the Church of England; adjusting for the missing parishes, there are probably 15,760 adult worshippers on any Sunday and 11,400 children. While the Dioceses of Birmingham, London and Southwark account for the majority of the black Anglican participation within the Church, it must be noted that every diocese has some black Anglican worshippers. The survey also identified the fact that black Anglicans bring a higher proportion of children to church: nationally there are 10 children for every 41 adults in church on a Sunday; among black worshippers, the ratio is 10 children to 16 adults.

However, many black Anglicans were not registering on the electoral rolls, and non-membership of electoral rolls may be one reason why they were numerically under-represented on PCCs and synods (my emphasis). In parishes where there are black Anglicans, they make up 4.5 percent of usual attendance, on average, but only 3 per cent of the electoral roll. In the same parishes, 4.4 per cent of the churchwardens are black and 3.4 per cent are PCC members. Churchwardens are elected by everyone in the parish, while PCC members and deanery synod representatives are elected only by those on the electoral roll. The question remains as to why all black Anglicans are not on electoral rolls?

Given the role of incumbents in parishes, CMEAC was very disappointed at the responses given by some to the survey questionnaire. There were incumbents who wrote quite disparagingly and some portrayed the survey as divisive:

- I try to be friendly and to help all of them, and the colour of their skin is as irrelevant as the coats they are wearing;

- We are colour blind in this parish and therefore treat this form with the contempt it deserves;

- When does black cease to be black and become coffee, brown, chocolate etc. etc?;

- Until this questionnaire I had not even considered racial identity as important. It isn't, I will not co-operate with this kind of mischief-making statistical analysis – so why this? There are approximately 2,500 souls in this benefice. Any Seeds of Hope for this parish will fall on stony ground until some black leadership emerges.

The question might well be asked to what extent were vicars really helping black leadership to emerge? It was quite clear that there was a great deal of educational work to be done in the parishes.

On the whole there were positive responses to the survey, and many not only completed the questionnaire but also supplied additional information. Some vicars were glad that the Committee had raised the issues and were looking forward to the results and recommendations, while several were concerned about the need for black participation and leadership at the national level of the church. They commented on the absence of black clergy and the need for vocations to ordained ministry.

With respect to good practice:

- one vicar spoke of the increase in the number of black young adults attending church and the likelihood of a black person being elected on to the PCC;
- another reported that their parish audit was taking place and multi-racial issues were firmly on the agenda;
- one parish was hoping to employ a full-time Christian Asian worker and was asking for the committee's fullest support and prayers;
- another vicar wished us well in our quest for the truth.
- The genuine concerns of many vicars might best be reflected in a comment by one: 'The Asian and Afro-Caribbean worshippers at St John's are part of the worship and work of the Church ... they are being harnessed as links between the Church and their ethnic groups in the parish'; the point was made by another vicar that our Church of England's capacity to affirm black people may reflect our success/failure as a Church.[4]

Among the Church's ministry, the survey found 92 black clergy, 39 lay readers and 17 Church Army Officers, as well as 536 eucharistic assistants and 673 group leaders. Within the Church's structures there were 213 black church wardens, 1,654 members of Parochial Church Councils, 237 members of Deanery Synods, 38 members of Diocesan Synods and 2092 sidesmen and women.

The *How We Stand* statistical survey provided a breakdown of dioceses and parishes where there were black Anglicans and that was extremely useful in encouraging a good attendance of black Anglicans at the Celebration. The survey showed that black people were worshipping in every diocese and participating at various levels of the Church. I remember there was one diocese which rang and said they would have to bring someone from a Pentecostal church because there were no black Anglicans. I remarked that a lack of black Anglicans could be embarrassing for them so I would send a print out of parishes where they were worshipping. The information proved very useful in identifying black Anglicans in that diocese as well as other dioceses that were having difficulty locating black Anglicans.

The survey report was extremely helpful in many ways:

1. it was quite clear that there was a great deal of educational work to be done with the clergy and in parishes;

2. no longer could people doubt the presence of black Anglicans – they were a presence throughout the Church and not just in London, Birmingham and Southwark;

3. we were able to identify the need to encourage black Anglicans to register on the electoral roll as that would give them access to the structures if they wished to be involved;

4. such a comprehensive survey helped to build further the Committee's credibility;

5. the Committee was in a position to identify the number of persons in various vocations within the Church, and the categories where there was the need to encourage more vocations. Although prior to the survey the Committee had some idea of the existing situation it was important to get hard facts;

6. the survey proved useful as a tool not only to the committee but also to the dioceses.

> It is often said that 'there are no black or white people in our congregation but only Christian people'. It is a laudable statement at one level but it denies people their social and cultural background and moreover it often hides or obscures the limitations or blind spots of the dominant cultural outlook. I believe that as a Church we must take culture more seriously for everyone's sake. It is part of being a Church of Pentecost, a Church in which so many more people are able to hear the mighty works of God in their own language.[5]

The Revd Lorraine Dixon (British-born of Jamaican origin) also states that:

> The concept of ethnicity is denied as a lived experience by statements such as 'I don't see you as Black' or 'I don't see colour, I just see people'. However this notion of colour blindness is put forward, the result is the same: 'I am not seen!' This process occurs within a context that suggests that minority ethnic people are inferior and represses their participation and visibility.[6]

chapter 10

The development of the Diocesan Network

> Let your gifts and calling be recognised and affirmed, our partnership in the life of the Church of England be evident and welcome. We seek to walk confidently in Christ, one in him with all of every ethnic group, tribe and tongue who name his name.[1]

This was one of the most exciting areas of work because it meant going out and engaging with people in order to develop an effective network. The Diocesan Network helped the Committee to get its message out to the dioceses and parishes. Meetings were hosted by the Committee's Chairman and were held twice per year on Saturdays. They were well-attended, joyous occasions, a time of sharing information and building confidence.

I felt that this network would be critical to the success of the Committee's work for many reasons, not least because *Faith in the City* had reported that there were repeated calls for the Church of England to 'make space for' and so better receive the gifts of black Christians. If this was really going to happen the Committee needed to be sure that it could identify competent and confident black Anglicans who would be willing to come forward and be involved with the structures at all levels.

The Diocesan Link Persons (DLPs) network originated in 1989 after the failure of the GS debate. Chapter 4 makes reference to their raison d'etre (see p. 28). In order to emphasize their role in the dioceses, as well as the link with the Committee, they agreed the following:

1. to get recommendations and issues which are being raised by CMEAC into the processes of dioceses, deaneries and parishes of dioceses;

2. to ensure that the Committee knows the issues in your diocese which are causing anxiety to the minority ethnic community and minority ethnic Anglicans in particular;

3. to organize a support group and make sure that at least one member is a young person, and that the group reflects the diversity in the diocese; to maybe meet once per month, raise issues of concern to the minority

ethnic community, and to consider what should the Church be doing. Young minority ethnic people tend to see the minority ethnic community as a community of failure, so highlight individual achievement and success. *Open doors to young minority ethnic people and offer support to help them to find who they are, as against who they think they are;*

4. to educate and encourage minority ethnic people to become involved at all levels of the Church;

5. to try to raise the profile of minority ethnic issues in the Church;

6. to arrange regional meetings of Link Persons;

7. to inform CMEAC's Secretary of good practice, so that information can be shared widely.

The number of dioceses represented among DLPs has fluctuated between 35 and 43. When informed of vacancies the committee has written to diocesan bishops who have been prompt about finding replacements. Although the network was set up really to help build confidence among the black Anglicans, there have been occasions when white people have come as diocesan representatives. This ensures that dioceses which have not been able to locate suitable black Anglicans will still be kept informed.

It was clear that mainly older people who had come from Africa, Asia or the Caribbean were involved as DLPs. In an effort to reach out to younger people and especially black British (between 18–35 years old) the Committee approached the diocesan bishops for nominees. These were nominated by the bishops in consultation with the Diocesan Link Persons. Usually between 20–23 dioceses are represented in the group. In course of time they adopted a logo, and they decided to call themselves 'Joynt Hope', both ideas supplied by Mrs Jennifer Edwards, one of their members. Despite the fact that Diocesan Network meetings are held on Saturdays, some young members find it difficult to attend because of other commitments.

Meeting expenses (travel and meal costs) are covered either by the Committee, or the Committee with financial assistance from diocesan bishops. We have had speakers on themes such as exclusions from schools, USPG and its tercentenary and the Commonwealth Secretariat. The meetings provide an opportunity for hearing about the Committee's work, as well as sharing information about what the dioceses are doing. The mood at the first few meetings was one of complaints about the racism in the Church and society. Since then there has been a change – despite the problems members are helping to find solutions and developing confidence. The network is well established as the group has come of age.

By 1993, I was able to publish the first edition of *Feedback*, a biannual newsletter for the network. Its purpose would be twofold:

1. To supply information on good practice which is being carried out in dioceses, deaneries and parishes as a follow up to *Seeds of Hope*.
2. To provide the network with a forum for gathering information about what is happening in their dioceses.

In the beginning all Diocesan Network meetings were held in Church House. Within recent times invitations extended by Diocesan Link Persons to hold meetings in their dioceses have been gladly accepted. The network visited Norwich, Liverpool and Canterbury dioceses (each with a purpose – Norwich to attend the Africa Day Service; Liverpool to meet with Bishop David Sheppard and visit the Merseyside Maritime Museum Slave Exhibition; and Canterbury to attend the launch of the Committee's report entitled *Simply Value Us: Meeting the Needs of Young Minority Ethnic Anglicans)*. Members often remark that they leave the meetings feeling energized and inspired.

Figure 5: Some of the Diocesan Network with the Rt Revd Dr Wilfred Wood, Bishop of Croydon, on the steps of Church House (1989)

The Diocesan Network has been a strong support to the Committee. They are all volunteers who give their valuable time generously to attend network meetings, consult with key people in the dioceses, encourage candidates for GS and other elections, spearhead race relations work in the dioceses, attend regional and national conferences and some serve as team members on the Committee's Advisory Team visits to dioceses.

This is a well-established, significant network and a wonderful asset to the Committee's work. I was able to draw on the network and offer names of persons to serve on national committees and working parties. Building up the Diocesan Network has been a real joy and members have been an inspiration to me.

In order to tap more into this resource, the Committee needs to do the following: to gather information about their expertise, interest and gifts through the setting up of a new database; as people serve and move on it is important to get in replacements through the good office of the bishops; through the Youth Issues Sub-Committee efforts should be made to increase the membership of Joynt Hope.

chapter 11

The development of CMEAC's youth work

- A lot of the time I ask the question what is my identity? I am Asian but not Muslim and Christian but not white, where do I fit in the community?

- The Church, should tackle institutional racism: develop a strategy for dealing with racism in parishes, Youth groups and schools.

- The Church needs to become more welcoming, accepting and be aware of different cultures and their needs.

- When we are outside the Church they want us to be in the Church, when we are in the Church they do not know what to do with us.[1]

In many respects the Black Anglican Youth Association (BAYA), was the forerunner to CBAC's youth work. With the support of the ABC and ACCM, the Association held Young Gifted and Black weekends in the 1980s. These were mainly for the purpose of fostering vocations. Members were nearly all born in Britain or brought up here. BAYA's agenda also included issues of culture, history and identity.

In 1988, Miss Rosemarie Dixon, chair of BAYA was invited to speak to CBAC about their aims and aspirations. The Committee felt that it was important to encourage and support BAYA as a forum for young black Anglicans and wanted to ascertain the best way to support the Association in its application for modest funds.

A small group of dedicated young, and not so young, persons were the organizers of BAYA. It was clear that they had been a dynamic group but the strain of having the same people take responsibility for the management was beginning to affect the Association. Added to that some young people were studying and concentrating on their careers so they found it difficult to be regular in their attendance. Sadly this eventually led to the petering out of BAYA's work.

CBAC realized that it would be necessary to meet with young people prior to the 1994 Celebration, so that their involvement could be encouraged. Consequently in 1992, the Committee held a meeting for young people, including some members of BAYA. The Committee was disappointed at the attendance (16 out of 43 dioceses were represented), however their enthusiasm, clarity, vitality and confidence made up for the lack of numbers. I remember our first meeting in Church House and the reactions of the young people – they could not believe that they had been invited to a meeting in that place, some were thrilled at meeting the first black bishop in the Church of England (one young woman went up and touched Bishop Wilfred), and were also happy to meet other young black Anglicans from mainly rural dioceses. They displayed a variety of talents and gifts and spoke honestly about their views and concerns about the church. Many spoke about the fellowship and hope which they felt in hearing of the Committee's work and meeting with other black Anglicans.

The CMEAC Youth Issues Sub-Committee

Initially, the Youth Issues Sub-Committee was chaired by the Revd Canon Hendrickse, CMEAC member, in 1996 he was succeeded by Ms Smitha Prasadam.

The sub-committee decided on three objectives based on issues raised by young people through the Celebration workshops, as well as other discussions with them:

1. to identify the needs of young black Anglicans;

2. to plan a programme which would attempt to address those needs;

3. to acquire resources in order to carry out the programme of work.

This programme has focused mainly on training, conferences, events, project support, networking and information. The Youth Issues Sub-Committee has been very fortunate in getting financial assistance annually from a grant given by the Department for Education and Employment to the GS Board of Education for youth work. Membership of the CMEAC Youth Issues Sub-Committee has always included one of the national youth officers, initially the Revd Jonathon Roberts, and his successor Mr Peter Ball. Both officers were very helpful and I always felt comfortable about seeking their advice. This sub-committee has been a small dedicated group, at least one member is from the original BAYA – Miss Cynthia Sutherland.

Programme of work

1. Training

- Training courses in communications offered annually by the Communications Unit.
- Financial assistance to young people pursuing training in youth work.

2. Conference participation

- Involvement in local, regional, national and international conferences. This section provides a sample of the Youth participation in events.

The Afro-Anglicanism Conference on 'Identity, Integrity and Impact in the Decade of Evangelism' was held in Capetown, South Africa from 18–25 January 1995. Six young people were included in the nineteen-member delegation from the Church of England viz.
Miss Rachel Smith, Miss Josile Munro, Sister Patsy Peart, Miss Caulene Herbert, Ms Smitha Prasadam, and the Revd Everton Mc Leod.

Delegates came from Brazil, Panama, USA, Alaska, the West Indies, including Haiti, Costa Rica, Papua New Guinea, Mauritius, Madagascar, Kenya, Nigeria, Rwanda, Tanzania, Uganda, Zaire, Burundi, the Sudan, West, Central and Southern Africa and England.

For most of the CMEAC delegation it was our first experience of visiting Africa. There were many unforgettable memories – the hospitality of the parishioners who took us in to their homes in Capetown, Pretoria and Johannesburg; the warmth and love of the people in townships despite their suffering under the oppressive apartheid regime from which they were emerging; the discussions and exchange of ideas among delegates from the wider Anglican community; meeting Archbishop Tutu; visiting Robben Island; and the beauty of South Africa especially Capetown; and in Egypt the generosity of spirit displayed by Bishop Ghias Malik, Bishop in Egypt, and the Revd Samy, Bishop's Chaplain. The conference and the visits to South Africa and Egypt were wonderfully enriching experiences.

The conference report was compiled mainly by the young people and other members of the delegation. On receipt of a copy, Canon Harold Lewis ECUSA Officer and Conference Co-ordinator requested several more copies because he was so impressed with the report. It is worthy of note that at that international conference, only the Church of England delegation had young participants. Appendix 9 provides the report's recommendations to the General Synod.

CMEAC members were provided with copies of the report and some members of the delegation addressed the Committee. Donors who had helped to finance the young delegates were sent copies of the report, i.e. both archbishops, the General Synod's Board of Education, the Central Church Fund, the Board of Mission, the USPG and the Church Army. The Partners in World Mission (PWM) invited CMEAC's Secretary to present the report and recommendations to their Committee. This was arranged by Mr John Clark who was then Secretary to PWM.

• The Second European Ecumenical Assembly (EEA II) held in Graz, Austria in 1997. I was able to procure funding for three young people to accompany me, Ms Josile Munro, Ms Smitha Prasadam and Mr Richard Ruddock.

• Capt. Rayman Khan, Ms Smitha Prasadam and Miss Anne-Marie Parker served as members of the Planning Group of the 'The Time of Our Lives', the Archbishop of Canterbury's 1999 Youth Conference.

• Code 2000: Mr James Orotayo, the Bishop of Lichfield's nominee on the CMEAC Youth Network, was invited to attend the mid-point conference which was held to review the Decade of Evangelism in the Anglican Communion. This was held in Kanuga, North Carolina, USA from 4th–9th September 1995. The Revd Canon John Sentamu, the Committee's Chairman, planned the worship material for the conference. This was drawn from all the liturgies of the Anglican Communion.

• CMEAC has been giving financial assistance to the annual Youth Conference held by the Southwark Race Relations Commission; financial support was also provided for regional conferences in Manchester and Sheffield as young people were involved.

• Mr Deo Meghan DLP for Coventry Diocese held a successful youth conference in September 1996, the theme of which was 'Youth with a Vision'. Participants from the Dioceses of Birmingham, Coventry, Oxford, Peterborough, Southwark and Winchester attended. CMEAC financed that event.

• Attendance and involvement in the General Synod Young Observer Group has not been good, a bigger effort will be needed to encourage involvement.

• The CMEAC's Youth Issues Sub-Committee together with the Vocations Sub-Committee held two vocations conferences in 1998 and 1999. More will be said on these in the section on vocations.

• Two members were invited by the youth officer to join a writers' group in order to prepare a Youth Sunday resources pack on racial justice.

Resources

CMEAC was grateful for the annual grant given by the Board of Education towards its youth work. As the Committee's programme of work progressed it became obvious that I would need someone to assist me with the youth work, because there was a great deal to be done in support of the Youth Issues Sub-Committee's agenda, and also in response to youth issues on the wider scene. The Chairman and members of the sub-committee were doing as much as they were able to but someone was needed in the office to assist us in this vital growing area of work. I approached Ms Anne-Marie Parker (British-born of Ghanaian origin), member of the GS Young Adult Observer Group about the possibility of giving some voluntary assistance. She agreed to do so for one year. I will always be grateful to Anne-Marie for her efforts which did advance the Committee's youth work. She carried out a number of initiatives: she developed a database of minority ethnic young people, published a newsletter 'Represent', assisted with planning the second Vocations Youth Conference and was involved in planning the Archbishop of Canterbury's 'Time of Our Lives Conference'. CMEAC hired her as a consultant to plan the launch of the report *Simply Value Us: Meeting the Needs of Young Minority Ethnic Anglicans*.

In the end, Anne-Marie worked with me over a two-year period. She had succeeded in developing a good network of young people both inside and outside the Church. In fact some of the contacts which Anne-Marie made were helpful to the youth research project.

Youth research project

In the meantime, with the approval of CMEAC and the assistance of the Youth Issues Sub-Committee a project proposal for a development worker was prepared as the Committee would not be able to employ someone on its existing budget. CMEAC applied to the Church Urban Fund's Development Fund for financial assistance. They felt that the project had potential but that the Committee needed to do some research in order to get young people's views. We went back to the drawing board, revised the proposal and applied for a second time, following which we were successful.

Between 1999–2000, the Youth Issues Sub-Committee concentrated mainly on the research project. Mrs Cynthia Poonam-Knight was employed to conduct the research and CMEAC was pleased with the outcome as the report entitled *Simply Value Us: Meeting the Needs of Young Minority Ethnic Anglicans* documented some very useful insights.

The aims of the research project were:

- to explore ways in which the Church of England is currently meeting the needs of young people from minority ethnic groups, both within the church and in the wider community;
- to create a portfolio of 'best practice';
- to identify unmet needs and suggest ways of developing the Church of England's work to meet the needs of young minority ethnic Anglicans.[2]

The Bishop of Dover (on the suggestion of Mrs Naomi Lumutenga, DLP for Canterbury Diocese), invited the Diocesan Network to hold the network meeting in Canterbury in June 2000. The Committee accepted the invitation and felt that it would be a good opportunity to launch the *Simply Value Us* report. CMEAC invited the Bishop of Dover to launch the report and he agreed. A few days before the event we were informed that the bishop could not attend as his diary was double-booked. This was very disappointing news, but the Bishop's Chaplain was able to attend. The Committee was very grateful to Mrs Angela Sarkis, Chief Executive of CUF, who agreed at short notice to launch the report.

The meeting was held at the new Education Centre located on the grounds of Canterbury Cathedral and the day's event was very successful. Over seventy people attended and most were young people from the Dioceses of Canterbury, London, Lichfield, Manchester, Oxford, Southwark and Winchester. This event was very inspiring and it left me feeling that there was still a lot of hope for the Church of England as there were minority ethnic young people who wanted to remain within the Church. However, how long will they remain if they are treated with indifference?

- I found the conference very interesting and inspiring.
- We are from different backgrounds, but found the whole day challenging and useful.
- Please keep in touch on events concerning vocations.
- I thought that I was coming to see the cathedral but I have seen and experienced much more.
- It was nice to meet people from the rest of the country and listen to their views and understand some more about Christianity. I came here with a different perspective of the day and left with a definite plus.

- Although I am not a part of the Church of England I found today's event most useful. I am excited about the Church's progress.

This report, which was published in the wake of the Stephen Lawrence Inquiry Report, asked the Church of England to listen to the concerns of young minority ethnic Anglicans and to be committed to developing strategies for addressing these concerns. Among the issues which the report highlights are:

- Racism within the Church and encouraging minority ethnic 'inclusion' within the Church should not just be left to the individual church leaders' good intentions.
- A national policy of inclusiveness is needed, whereby the gifts that our young people bring are received by the Church.
- Chapter 6 of the report offers very positive recommendations to the national, diocesan (e.g. youth officers) and parish levels of the Church.

Together with the follow-up report to the Board of Education's *Youth A Part* report, the *Simply Value Us* report was presented at the General Synod 2000 July sessions. It was noticeable that when the debate was announced, for one reason or another, half the hall emptied as Synod members left although some did return eventually. I felt that this might have given the young people who were present the impression that their issues were of little importance in the eyes of many General Synod members. The following motions were passed by the General Synod:

1. that this Synod take note of the report and welcomes the positive work resulting from *Youth A Part*;
2. that this Synod commends those working at National, Diocesan and Parish level to:
   a) enable young people to make an active contribution to the mission of the Church, especially with regard to evangelism and social justice;
   b) actively encourage young people's participation in decision making in the Church and to reduce structural and cultural blocks which inhibit this, especially with reference to minority ethnic concerns;
   c) secure resources to enable young people to be active in the Church's mission.

The *Simply Value Us* report highlighted several needs and underlined the importance of appointing a Youth Development Worker. Once more that raised the question of funding so that proper staff support could be employed.

Future of the work

In 2001, Captain Rayman Khan, youth officer in the Southwark Diocese and current Chairmain of CMEAC's Youth Issues Sub-Committee, presented to them, as well as CMEAC, a draft proposal for the future of youth work. He is in the process of consultation with Diocesan Youth Officers and other interested persons. This project has potential and should be given the blessings and support of all those who could make a difference. Whereas in the past the strategy was mainly a 'top down' approach, this new proposal is suggesting a 'bottom up' strategy. Maybe both strategies working in collaboration would be even more effective.

chapter 12
The development of vocations

It seems highly unlikely that God is not calling minority ethnic people to be ordained in the Church …[1]

The panel was informed that minority ethnic Anglicans feel they have to work up to three times as hard as their white counterparts to succeed by this process, and that by and large, young people from minority ethnic communities do not see ministry as a vocation for them.[2]

Disaffected and distressed on arrival we left the conference cherished in the sight of God and eager to 'go forth and tell'.[3]

My concern is that although young people from minority ethnic backgrounds bring a unique gift of ministry to the Church and the wider society, yet they are not encouraged to take up positions of leadership and service. What our Church needs in this millennium is a more culturally diverse lay and ordained leadership.

The reports of the Leicester Consultation (1981), the Balsall Health Consultation (1986) and the 1994 Black Anglican Celebration all speak of the importance of encouraging vocations from minority ethnic Anglicans. *Faith in the City* spoke of the removal of barriers particularly in relationship to ordained ministry. The Black Anglican Youth Association through their conferences had promoted vocations. Added to that, through a survey of black clergy carried out by the Revd Rajinder Daniel in the early years, and *How We Stand*, a later survey report, it was clear that a great deal more effort was needed if there was to be an increase in minority ethnic vocations. The Committee therefore decided to place this matter at the centre of its work. *The 1996 revised Terms of Reference stated under these terms of reference the work of the Committee will include in paragraph vi. Seeking the development and empowerment of minority ethnic Anglicans and in particular fostering and encouraging vocations within the Church.* By 1997, the CMEAC Vocations Sub-Committee was set up under the chairmanship of the Revd Charles Lawrence, a Committee member. The membership included mainly persons who represented lay and ordained ministries within the Church.

The Sub-Committee started its work with a Day of Prayer and Reflection which was led jointly by Canon Smith-Cameron and Mr Charles Severs. A number of issues were raised in the brainstorming session during that day, for instance it was clear that given the role of the Advisory Board of Ministry with respect to vocations, further collaboration with them would be a matter of urgency.

Discussions with ABM

Discussions were held with Archdeacon Gordon Kuhrt, Chief Secretary of ABM on issues such as vocations, theological education and training in racism awareness, ethnic monitoring of candidates, deployment of minority ethnic clergy, the training of selectors and DDOs, and ethnic monitoring of Readers. This in turn led to discussions with the Revd Roy Screech, Senior Selection Secretary on the training of selectors.

- The Vocations Sub-Committee was requested to review the Selectors' Handbook as well as the Diocesan Director of Ordinands' Handbook in an effort to ensure that 'race' issues were properly identified.

- With respect to minority ethnic selectors, on at least two occasions with the support of ABM, the Committee had written to diocesan bishops about the importance of having minority ethnic people among their selectors.

- The Chairman of the Vocations Sub-Committee was a member of the ABM's Vocations Advisory Panel.

- The Sub-Committee was asked to review ABM's ethnic monitoring form. Following that the Revd Screech reported that with respect to the ethnic monitoring form, the following had been agreed:

    The ethnic monitoring form continued to be used for all candidates sponsored by Selection Conference; annual statistics were compiled on the number of candidates attending Selection Conferences and the numbers recommended and not recommended (UK white and all others); comparative numbers of those who enter training each year, withdraw from training each year, and the number in training each year; figures were reported to the Recruitment and Selection Committee (RSC) and the Committee on Black Anglican Concerns; ABM's Annual Report would contain a précis of these figures.

- On behalf of CMEAC, the Revd Charles Lawrence wrote a paper on 'Structure and Funding of Ordination Training to that Working Party'.

- The Revd Mark Sowerby, Vocations Officer, was invited to serve on the Vocations Sub-Committee. The Revd Stephen Ferns, his successor, has become a member of the Sub-Committee.

I will comment on theological education later in this report. The role of theological colleges and courses is of paramount importance and cannot be overlooked because they are responsible for the training of all ordinands.

Other areas of the vocations sub-committee's work

- A survey of minority ethnic ordinands in theological colleges, courses and schemes was carried out by Bishop David Gillett, member of Vocations Sub-Committee, and member of CMEAC.

- Question posed by Bishop David to the GS on the training for ordinands in relation to racism awareness.

- Non-Stipendiary Ministry as it relates to minority ethnic Anglicans was discussed with the Revd Andrew Davey, BSR's Community and Urban Affairs Committee Officer, in relation to the GS publication *Stranger in the Wings: A Report on Local Non-Stipendiary Ministry.*

- Discussion with Captain Hugh Boorman, Candidates' Secretary for the Church Army on vocations.

- Discussion with the Revd George Kovoor, Chairman of CMEAC's Asian Anglican sub-Committee on concerns related to 'Vocations and Asian Anglicans'.

- Mr Charles Severs presented a paper on 'Vocations in Relationship to Religious Communities'.

The 1998 and 1999 Vocations Conferences

The Sub-Committee organized jointly with CMEAC's Youth Issues Sub-Committee Vocations Conferences in 1998 and 1999. Although the numbers were small the conferences meant a great deal to those who attended.

The Vocations Conferences were supported by the Ministry Division. Archdeacon Kuhrt, the Revd Mark Sowerby and Mrs Margaret Sentamu (now Senior Selection Secretary) made substantial contributions to them. The report entitled *Serving God in Church and Community: Vocations for Minority Ethnic Anglicans in the Church of England* (2000) provides a real insight into the views of participants (1998 and 1999) and how the Church perceives them. One woman who wanted to explore ordained ministry was told by the DDO that ministry was only for English people. Is it any wonder that the diversity in our pews is not reflected in ministry? By the end of the weekend participants left full of hope and empowered. Some are currently in training for ordination and one person went on for training in youth work.

The *Serving God* report includes a Foreword by Archbishop George Carey and Archbishop David Hope, together with messages of support from Archdeacon Kuhrt, as well as the three minority ethnic bishops in the Church of England: Bishop Nazir-Ali, Bishop John Sentamu and Bishop Wilfred Wood.

The conference report and recommendations are seeking more positive action and support from diocesan bishops, DDOs, vocations advisers, parish clergy and higher education chaplains to encourage minority ethnic vocations. The letter from the Revd Rose Huson-Wilkin, Chair of CMEAC, includes questions for discussion by the dioceses. *Exploring vocation starts at the parish level and parish clergy especially need to be aware of their responsibility in this regard.*

Ordained ministry - a revolving door?

I have heard and seen many times over the pain expressed by minority ethnic clergy who have been hurt and disillusioned by the attitude of church wardens, the PCC, the archdeacon, and sometimes that of the bishop. Most white parishes do not wish to accept black priests, they find it difficult to accept their authority. Minority ethnic priests are given a hard time, and yet as in the case of other priests they are trained to minister to the whole Church and not just parishes with a majority of minority ethnic people. The issues are complex and cannot be aired or dealt with in this report. *I seek to raise it because this is an unresolved matter which needs to be honestly and properly discussed in terms of the support which the Church should offer to minority ethnic clergy. Any discussion should include key people within the structures as well as representatives from the Association of Black Clergy.*

Clergy will make mistakes – whether minority or majority ethnic clergy – because they are human beings, yet minority clergy are pressured and are expected to be three times as good as majority ethnic clergy. They often find it difficult not only to get employment but also sometimes serve a longer period of curacy.

Even though I was trained in England and was 29 years old when I was ordained it was twelve years before I had a parish of my own. Two parishes turned me down. I wrote letters to several bishops. None of them asked to see me. Their reply was, I would be considered when they next had a vacancy. But I never heard from any of them again.[4]

Older minority ethnic clergy, despite all the hardship, for the most part will stay and continue in ministry, although some do go off into sector ministry – hospital, prison and university chaplaincies. The younger clergy faced with racism at every stage will not remain. It is hard work to get them to consider ordained ministry and after a few years they leave because it becomes unbearable. I know of at least three cases where young clergy have left without a trace because they were so utterly disillusioned that they did not wish to be contacted by the Church. The question to be posed is: Until the Church of England 'cleans up its act' should we be putting minority ethnic Anglicans through this appalling situation? Yet where minority ethnic clergy are supported and helped by the structures they do remain and give credible service to God's glory.

There is a whole agenda to be set with respect to nurturing vocations among minority ethnic Anglicans. The Committee will have to lead on this challenge and draw in people such as Mrs Sentamu, who has presented a paper on vocations to the Stephen Lawrence Follow-Up Group, and also get the views of its Vocations Sub-Committee and the Association of Black Clergy. The Diocese of Southwark has set up a programme to encourage vocations and can be consulted through the Diocesan CMEAC.

> The church needs to set a long-term strategy of 10 to 20, even 30 years of either trying to woo back minority ethnic Christians who were baptised Anglicans, or better still, to nurture the present young people who are in our churches.[5]

The Committee is proposing to host a conference entitled 'Serving God in Church and Community: Clergy Conference on Minority Ethnic Vocations', in order to enhance and encourage good practice among the clergy. The Archbishops' Council has given its approval for the event. The House of Bishops is aware of the conference and the Ministry Division is giving its support. CMEAC is planning to have an attendance of approximately 250 participants which will include parish clergy, lay leaders, chaplain and sector ministers, as well as some bishops, DDOs, theological college personnel, and ecumenical experts. The objectives will be as follows:

1. To examine good practice in promoting vocations to ordained and lay ministries and the vocation to be a Christian, and to explore how that could be used and adapted in a variety of situations.

2. To support and affirm the work which is already being done by clergy and lay leaders, and to encourage dioceses and parishes which need to be doing work in this area.

3. To examine ways in which the church can be pro-active in the area of minority ethnic vocations within its general life.

4. To support and affirm minority ethnic clergy.

5. To encourage every diocese to have a strategy for how it includes vocations for minority ethnic Anglicans in the widest sense – and to set achievable objectives.

chapter 13
Asian Anglican concerns

In 1995, the Partners' in World Mission (PWM) Committee with the support of the Board of Mission and CMEAC held an Asian Anglican Consultation in order to hear and discuss their concerns. The consultation report was presented to CMEAC by Canon Smith-Cameron and Mr John Clark, Secretary PWM.

CMEAC decided to set up a sub-committee which would address specifically the concerns of Asian Anglicans, chaired by the Revd George Kovoor. The membership included people such as Mr Robin Thomson (Training, Research and Outreach to South Asians in the UK, South Asia and the Diaspora) and Mr John Clark (who represented the Board of Mission and PWM).

We discussed issues such as perceptions, leadership, involvement, vocations, converts, youth, social and racial justice, liturgical issues (e.g. the use of Asian languages), and cultures. Although they were clearly areas of common concern with other minority ethnic Anglicans, there were distinct and particular concerns relevant to Asian Anglicans. Members felt that the matter of conversion and support was not being properly addressed by the Church and that was a particular area in which the sub-committee could make a contribution.

By 1999, the sub-committee decided to host a weekend conference which would have as its theme 'Conversion and the Church of England: Asian Experiences'. The main aim would be to encourage the Church to welcome and affirm those who come to Christ from other faith backgrounds.

The conference was held from 17–19 September 1999 at Crowther Hall, Birmingham, where the Revd Kovoor is the Principal. There were 21 participants of whom 16 had converted to Christ from other faith backgrounds. Almost all were Asian participants of Indian, Pakistan, Sri Lankan, Japanese, Korean, Malaysian and Guyanese origins, and included both first and second-generation British Asians. Conference support was provided by Crowther Hall, the Board of Mission, PWM and CMEAC.

Through the telling of stories, the process of conversion was discussed – factors that attracted people and factors which put people off, e.g. the sense of peace and God's presence; the language of the Church appeared to be unnecessarily exclusive. Converts spoke about the high cost of conversion and often a sense of isolation because they were ostracized from their families and cultures. Participants spoke of conversion as a process with stages, every day was part of the conversion experience. They recounted their experiences in the Church of England – some felt embraced by the Church and community and included in a family which showed practical love.

All had negative experiences in varying degrees ranging from coldness and indifference to explicit rejection. In most cases this was connected with their minority ethnic background and cultural differences. One person described the reaction when she wore her shalwar kaneez (Punjabi dress) to church: some of the members felt threatened, as though 'you are going to take over our church...' The sense of rejection was all the more painful for those who had experienced a break from their family.

> The conference ended on a positive note with a list of guidelines, for a local church to reach out to people of other faiths, also a list of issues and recommendations for the Church of England.[1]

It has been a disappointment that the report has not been published especially because these are 'live' issues, also because conference participants expressed some frustration that it had taken so long to follow up on the earlier PWM consultation with Asian Christians. The plan is that there is the intention to organize a bigger conference. The outcome of that event together with the first report will enable a more substantial conference report. Again Crowther Hall is willing to play a leading role in planning that event in collaboration with CMEAC.

Part 5

The response by the Church of England's structures 1991–2001

chapter 14

The Passing Winter: A Sequel to Seeds of Hope and the Parish Study Pack

Looking at Diocesan Boards and Committees, is this the way to celebrate God's diversity? Why are we in this Church?[1]

... that all diocesan senior staff meetings submit themselves to racism awareness training. This should include Diocesan Secretaries. Unless those responsible for managing the structures become aware of their racism, they cannot combat it.[2]

If the Church is a sign and fore taste of the coming Kingdom of God, it is high time that as a Church we openly stated our commitment to the rooting out of racism in our structures ... The presence of racism is as much to do with a lack of thinking as of hostility to our sisters and brothers. It is as much to do with our accepting the prevailing culture of the day as to do with complicity with evil. As Christians we are called to follow Christ and that involves doing new things, adopting new policies.[3]

We need more models locally ... we must beware of paternalism and tokenism, but we need to be working at encouraging those from minority ethnic Anglican groups to take their rightful place in the Councils of the Church at parish, deanery, diocesan and General Synod level.[4]

The Committee's monitoring role is one of its strengths which it has used assiduously in working with the structures to combat institutional racism. This responsibility is highlighted in CBAC's original Terms of Reference, as well as the revised versions in 1990 and 1996. The principal tasks of the Committee for Minority Anglican Concerns (CMEAC) will be to monitor issues arising, or which ought to arise, in the context of the work of the Archbishops' Council, the General Synod's boards and councils, and of the General Synod itself, as far as they have policy implications for minority ethnic groups within the Church and the wider community.

In 1992, the Committee's Chairman had presented a paper to the House of Bishops in relation to the follow-up to *Seeds of Hope*. It stated that the Committee would request diocesan progress reports from the dioceses in 1993 and 1994, as these would enable the committee to monitor the response to *Seeds of Hope* by dioceses, deaneries and parishes.

By 1993, in response to a questionnaire from the Committee's *Seeds of Hope* Advisory Group, twenty-six dioceses indicated that they were developing work, while an appreciable number of dioceses still did not consider this work as a matter of urgency or priority. The Advisory Group chaired by Prebendary Theo Samuel decided to request the second progress report in 1995 as this would give the dioceses more time to respond to the recommendations in *Seeds of Hope*. In 1995, when the exercise was repeated there was 100 percent response from the dioceses. This was reminiscent of the diocesan response to the survey questionnaire which produced the *Seeds of Hope* report.

The Advisory Sub-Committee felt that the outstanding response could have been due to several reasons:

- the relationship which CMEAC had developed with the House of Bishops whereby the committee consulted the Bishops on major pieces of work in advance in order to get their views and support;
- the commitment of the CMEAC Diocesan Network in encouraging the diocese;
- and not least the impact of the 1994 Black Anglican Celebration for the Decade of Evangelism.

In producing *The Passing Winter: A Sequel to Seeds of Hope*, CMEAC was attempting to fulfil the following tasks:

1. to record the progress made by the Church of England in the task of combating racism since the General Synod debate on the report in November 1991;
2. to provide an overview and understanding of how the work is being tackled by dioceses;
3. to provide examples of good practice which will be of value to other dioceses, deaneries and parishes;
4. to support those dioceses which are finding the task of addressing the issues hard going, also to encourage them to learn from dioceses of a similar profile which are tackling the issues effectively;

5. to identify further what the Church should be doing in order to give a positive and stronger response to the task of combating racism in its structures.[5]

The Passing Winter identified good practice at all levels of the Church, provided an overview of how the task of combating racism was being undertaken and identified further work which the Church of England should be doing in order to give a positive and stronger response to the task of combating racism.

The outgoing Committee took the decision that the new CMEAC should approve the final draft of *The Passing Winter* before it was published so that they would own the report. This was done in October 1996 at the first meeting of the new Committee. *The Passing Winter: A Sequel to Seeds of Hope* would also be debated by the General Synod in the new quinquennium (1995–2000).

The report was launched at a press conference on 12 November 1996 and debated at the General Synod sessions on 26 November 1996. The Rt Revd Dr John Sentamu, the Committee's Chairman and Bishop of Stepney opened the debate. In his speech, he spoke of:

> the steady progress which had been made, part of the encouraging landscape is the contribution made by the Church of England in its willingness to relate to issues of racial justice, both internally and externally, in the context of rising racism in the United Kingdom and the rest of Europe.[6]

He said that the Committee's task had been 'one of evidence-gathering in the past five years', and the evidence of the reports received from some of the dioceses shows that there remains a small hard-core of resistance which responds in this way: 'We have no black people here, there is no problem.' The Chairman acknowledged that a great deal more was required by way of education in deaneries and parishes. Bishop John asked members

> to give us practical suggestions related to the 27 recommendations in the report: recommendations which state the present hopeful positions of the Church of England and yet encourage us further to the ultimate goal of banishing racism from our institutions and systems. ... How could we bring this good progress to a successful conclusion? How could the culture of the Church of England be radically shifted and transformed?

General Synod members responded very positively and offered constructive suggestions on youth work, representation, liturgy, use of church buildings, equal opportunity, training institutions, laity development and adult education programmes, cultural awareness, use of language, school exclusions and Racial Justice Sunday.

The Passing Winter made 27 recommendations to the dioceses and their structures, to the parishes and the General Synod boards and councils.

The following motions were unanimously agreed by the General Synod:

1. that the Synod do take note of the Report;
2. that this Synod reaffirming its commitment to overcoming racism and welcoming the progress towards that end reported in GS 1220, commend the report, and in particular the recommendations in Chapter VI, for study and appropriate action by all parts of the Church.

Canon Hendrickse in his thesis analysed the tone and arguments of this debate with previous debates arising out of the Committee's work. He said that

> Sentamu had managed to make Synod feel worthy of itself as a Christian body and of the work it was undertaking ... The report and debate of *The Passing Winter* was remarkable in its achievements. It offered models of good practice and practical ways of dealing with racism in dioceses and parishes. By doing so it made those who exercised leadership at every level of the Church's life aware that there were ways of addressing the issue which were constructive, reconciling and progressive.

From my own perspective, whereas the General Synod debates in 1988, 1989 and 1991 indicated that there was still a denial that racism existed in the Church and an unwillingness by the Church as a corporate body to take up the challenge of combating racism, by 1996 we were beginning to discern a considerable shift in what the General Synod was saying. The speeches in that debate showed that the General Synod had moved on in its understanding of the issues, members displayed a willingness to begin to engage with 'race' issues, and to admit that there was work to be done by the Church, our Church. Bishop John's invitation asking members to give practical suggestions elicited a good response, as members came forward with very positive and practical suggestions. In fact when asked whether any GS members had been trained in racism awareness, whether through the Church or in their employment, there was an appreciable show of hands.

Five years on from the Seeds of Hope debate, the committee was able to report to the Synod, believing that there has been an emerging visibility of minority ethnic Anglicans since the committee was formed. Disappointingly, the committee also reported that there remained a hard core of resistance which still responds 'We have no black people here, there is no problem'. A reply such as this clearly indicates that the Church of England still has considerable ground to cover in addressing the issues through all its structures if this work is to be truly within the lifeblood of the Church's mission and ministry.[7]

The *Seeds of Hope in the Parish Study Pack*

This study pack was published shortly after *The Passing Winter* and is meant to be a companion document.

> Based on the analysis of the first and second diocesan progress reports, as well as the questionnaire replies from parishes to *How We Stand: A Report on Black Anglican Membership of the Church of England* in the 1990's, it was quite clear to the committee that many parishes had not yet put education on racism and racial justice issues on their agenda. This led to the decision to prepare a study pack. The Seeds of Hope Advisory Group undertook the task of writing the study pack, in a sensitive style so that parishioners would be willing to discuss the issues, and plan positive strategies for action. The pack suggests that the nature of God, the nature of humanity and the nature of the church should be used as a theological framework. The pack attempts to take the parish group/PCC meeting through a step-by-step approach in five sections. It includes questions for discussion, Bible study material, an act of worship, meanings of words which we use and a list of resources.[8]

In an effort to encourage dioceses, deaneries and parishes to do follow-up work with *The Passing Winter* as well as the *Seeds of Hope in the Parish Study Pack*, CMEAC did the following:

- By December 1996, Bishop John Sentamu wrote to diocesan bishops about their role in the follow-up to *The Passing Winter* GS debate. The letter offered concrete suggestions on how that could be done.

- CMEAC suggested that both publications should be sent to incumbents.

- Six complimentary copies of the study packs were sent to diocesan secretaries, together with correspondence encouraging them to photocopy and supply incumbents with the study pack.

- Correspondence and copies of *The Passing Winter*, as well as the study pack were also sent to suffragan bishops who were not members of GS; also to clergy, and lay chairmen of Diocesan Synods, as well as Diocesan Social Responsibility Officers.

- Correspondence and copies of both publications were sent to CMEAC's diocesan network.[9]

I will not present in this report information on good practice displayed by dioceses, deaneries and parishes as that is comprehensively recorded in *The Passing Winter* (1996), as well as in CMEAC's *Good Practice Paper for Dioceses* published in 2001.

chapter 15
The Passing Winter Advisory Team visits to dioceses

Thank you for your letter of 30th March together with your Committee's very substantial and helpful report. We shall work through your Report thoroughly and remain grateful that you and your colleagues have given so much time to the diocese of Derby. The visit itself, and now the Report have given all these issues a much higher profile.[1]

As I said on the telephone, I am most grateful for the excellent report produced by CMEAC. I hope that you sensed when you were here how much we enjoyed your visit, which was both stimulating and encouraging. Given the relatively short time you were here with us, I am amazed at the grasp of the realities of complicated issues that are revealed and the fullness and helpfulness of your recommendations.[2]

The *Seeds of Hope* Advisory Sub-Committee's work had culminated in the publishing of *The Passing Winter* and the *Seeds of Hope in the Parish Study Pack*. In 1996, after the GS debate on *The Passing Winter: A Sequel to Seeds of Hope*, Prebendary Theo Samuel resigned as Chairman so that someone else would be appointed to chair the new *Passing Winter* Advisory Sub-Committee. The Committee thanked Prebendary Samuel for his dedicated leadership in chairing the *Seeds of Hope* Advisory Sub-Committee.

CMEAC appointed the Revd Canon Clarry Hendrickse to undertake the task of chairing the new sub-committee which would monitor the Church's response to *The Passing Winter*. The new sub-committee continued with, and intensified the number of visits which were carried out to dioceses each year. This was in order to monitor their response to *The Passing Winter* and the study pack. The team targeted mainly rural dioceses as there was complacency and indifference to these issues in several of those areas.

By 2001, Advisory Teams had visited 36 dioceses (note Appendix 10). The following dioceses have not had team visits:

Canterbury	Sodor and Man
Ely	St Edmundsbury and Ipswich
Europe	Truro
Rochester	Worcester

The lack of staff meant revisits to dioceses were not possible, apart from the Diocese of London which we visited twice. I had to do follow-up work mainly through questionnaires. The CMEAC's responsibility to act as a support and resource to dioceses was taken seriously so that all requests for assistance (whether at the diocesan, deanery or parish level) were dealt with by the Committee members or the Committee's Secretary, as appropriate.

I was able to put together teams for diocesan visits (six people per team) because people were generous with their time despite the sacrifice to themselves. They believed in what the Committee was trying to achieve and so they were committed. Advisory Team visits were held over a two or three-day period. In an effort to meet with as many people as possible within the Church, as well as within secular/community based agencies, the team always had very busy schedules. The visit was always planned to coincide with the Bishop's Council meeting so that the Advisory Team would have the opportunity to reflect on some of what the team had heard and experienced. Following the visit, a detailed report with recommendations would be sent to the diocesan bishop for him to circulate, and discuss as appropriate.

The objectives of the visits were as follows:

1. to listen and learn;

2. to raise issues as appropriate;

3. to offer advice and support to the diocese with respect to the recommendations from *Seeds of Hope*, *The Passing Winter* and the *Seeds of Hope in the Parish Study Pack*;

4. to get some idea of how the diocese was responding to the Stephen Lawrence Inquiry Report.

I am extremely grateful to everyone who served on teams over the years; members were reliable about being on time and contributing positively to the team. There were only two occasions when we had absentees, once someone was very ill, and in another situation there was a death in the family. The task was a serious one and it was taken seriously, and a new team member would fit in very quickly and become part of the team. Although we worked long hours and sometimes were quite exhausted (e.g. the London visit in 2000 when we had to travel long distances by tube, which was often cancelled), we had our laughs! I felt privileged to have had the opportunity to attend all 36 visits to the dioceses as CMEAC's Secretary and as Secretary to the Advisory Teams. Although all members of one body, the Church of England, the dioceses are all quite different in their style of operation and often their structures. This was always taken into consideration in the report and recommendations that followed each diocesan visit.

This programme of work was very significant because it was casting a mirror on the dioceses, and providing a picture of how they were responding. I do hope that any new programme of work will include the advisory team visits because of the support which the committee is able to offer the dioceses through this strategy.

A Good Practice Paper for Dioceses (2001)

We have been greatly encouraged and supported by the dioceses in the high degree of commitment and detailed planning which is done in preparation for our visits.[3]

This is a clear strategy of the Committee to make available realistic and achievable practices. It is hoped that all who are themselves committed

Figure 6: A reception held by the Mayor of Carlisle in honour of an Advisory Team visit in 1997.

to a more inclusive church, will find within this paper some ready tools to begin their task.[4]

Despite the quite strongly held view that there is no racism in rural parishes, that some who hold this view constitute the so-called white highlands, and that increasing cultural diversity is not an issue for them, the reality can be different.[5]

The Committee recommends that within CME and POT there is an acknowledged responsibility to have racism awareness training, to challenge racism within parish communities and congregations and to raise awareness of racial justice issues.[6]

The Good Practice Paper for Dioceses was published and launched at a press conference in 2001. The paper was compiled out of the experience gained from CMEAC'S *Passing Winter* Advisory Team visits to dioceses, as well as the questionnaires which have been circulated to dioceses in order to follow-up mainly *The Passing Winter: A Sequel to Seeds of Hope* and *The Seeds of Hope in the Parish Study Packs.* Recently the issues of social cohesion in our nation have become increasingly vital. The onus on the Church to show within its own structures, policies and their implementation, that it is equipping itself to take part with integrity in the debate, is urgent. *The Good Practice Paper* is meant to assist dioceses in the Church of England and to encourage all dioceses to recommit themselves to the task of combating institutional racism.[7]

Objectives of the paper

1. To highlight good practice on various issues in dioceses, deaneries and parishes in order to inform other dioceses.

2. To identify policies in the Church of England which are attempting to combat institutional racism.

3. To provide information on resources which can be helpful to all dioceses in tackling institutional racism.

4. To highlight issues of relevance to dioceses, deaneries and parishes as raised in Bishop Sentamu's paper, and *Called to Lead: a challenge to include Minority Ethnic People.*

5. To encourage dioceses which have not attempted to address these issues to set up a programme of action.

6. To encourage other dioceses to redouble their efforts and develop systematic action plans.

The themes which have been presented (listed below) can help dioceses to develop an integrated and sustained approach in order to combat institutional racism. Those themes were constantly brought to the Committee's attention as areas in which guidance could be helpful. Each theme is accompanied by a question/s in order to prompt discussion and action.

A. Review of the diocese and its policies

    i) Review
   ii) Ethnic Monitoring
  iii) Diocesan motions
  iv) Constitutions/Terms of Reference
   v) Membership of Synods Boards, Councils and Committees
  vi) Equal Opportunities Policy

B. Racism
C. Education
D. Parish Education
E. Deaneries
F. Vocations
G. Training for clergy and other ministries
H. Racial Justice Sunday
I. The Cathedral
J. Resource Centres
K. Chaplaincies
L. Secular Agencies

During my sabbatical leave in 2001 I used the time to compile the report on behalf of CMEAC's *Passing Winter* Advisory sub-Committee, who had contributed towards its production.

chapter 16

Equal Opportunities Policy (EOP)

Equal Opportunities policies play an important part of combating racism and much work has gone into implementing a comprehensive policy within the national church institutions. The National Church Institutions (NCI) launched its Equal Opportunities Policy in January 2000 and also sent it to all dioceses, diocesan bishops and organisations allied to the Church (e.g. the Mothers' Union) ... so far (NCI) 500 staff have attended training.[1]

... and in the schools where I am governor we have learnt to take equal opportunities seriously and to realise that they give us new opportunities. However, they underpin everything that we do; they are not just a policy that we write and put on the shelf along with other policies; they need constant work in implementing training of all the people involved in an organisation; they need monitoring and evaluating.[2]

The Dioceses of Birmingham, Southwark and Chelmsford had formulated EOPs well ahead of Church House. In the first phase of the Committee's work I reported on the fact that the semblance of an EOP had been drafted but there was no further follow-up. With the arrival of Mr Phillip Mawer, the new Secretary General (he had been Secretary to the Scarman Report into the Brixton riots), matters took a turn for the better. Mr Mawer met with the staff of GS boards and councils, and with senior staff individually. At our meeting he asked me if there was one matter that I wanted addressed in Church House what would that be? My reply was that the staff should have an Equal Opportunities Policy. I remarked that it would be important for Church House, also it would send a powerful message to the dioceses about what they ought to be doing. The CBAC also asked Mr Mawer to place EOP high on the agenda.

Hence the EOP was revived and rewritten, and by 1993 after a great deal of consultation in house, as well as with external agencies, a comprehensive EOP (including a Monitoring Sheet) was ready for implementation. In order to ensure this first policy's effectiveness, an EOP Monitoring Group was set up chaired by the personnel officer. On an 'ongoing' basis training was provided as part of the orientation for new staff in Church House, as part of training for other staff, as well as for chairmen of interviewing panels.

The Committee believes that the Central Board of Finance's Equal Opportunities Policy helped some dioceses which used it as a model for preparing their own policies. The formulation of an EOP by the CBF, as well as some dioceses indicated that the task was manageable and not as daunting as it appeared to be.

In 1992 and 1995, the Committee wrote to diocesan secretaries in order to get an up-to-date picture on the extent to which dioceses had progressed in formulating and implementing their EOPs.

Dioceses fell into four categories:

1. dioceses with comprehensive policies
2. dioceses with brief statements
3. dioceses working on policies
4. dioceses without policies, most of whom judged there was no need.

We were getting remarks such as:

- 'After all we are Christians and would not be unjust';
- 'The bishop and staff responsible for appointments would not discriminate';
- 'There is no immediate intention of formulating or debating such a policy. Some dioceses saw equal opportunity only as a race issue';
- 'There are very few ethnic minority people who live in this diocese and there has never been an application from a member of an ethnic minority group for any jobs we have on offer'.

Through the good offices of Mr David Williams, Secretary of the Central Board of Finance, a team of three – Mr Christopher Ball, General Synod Office, Ms Rosemary Towler, Equal Opportunities Trainer and CMEAC's Secretary addressed the 1997 diocesan secretaries' annual residential conference.

The Conference noted that the drafting of an equal opportunities policy was only the beginning of the process and not an end in itself. There needed also to be a system for implementing and monitoring its implementation and parishes also needed to be encouraged to seriously consider the subject. The Conference also noted the potential effects of the Disability Discrimination Act on both dioceses and parishes in terms of buildings and services.

As a result of the Turnbull Report, there was restructuring at the national level of the Church, and that meant that certain policies were reviewed – including the EOP which had been designed in 1993 for Church House staff. By January 2000, a Joint Equal Opportunities Policy for the National Church Institutions – Staff of the Archbishops' Council, Bishopthorpe Palace, the Church Commissioners, Lambeth Palace and the Church of England Pensions Board was launched. The Joint EOP encompasses issues of gender, culture, colour, ethnic or national origin, nationality including citizenship, age, sexual orientation, disability, HIV status, social class, marital status, membership of a trade union and political status. A new Equal Opportunities Monitoring Group was set up to monitor the organizations' adherence to the policy, as well as to help them embrace the policy proactively. Harassment Advisers have been appointed, the recruitment and selection policy has been revised, and a complaints procedure put in place. The EOP Monitoring Group is chaired by the Director of Policy and includes representatives from BSR, ABM, the Board of Education, the Communications Unit, the Statistics Unit, the Director of Human Resources and CMEAC's Secretary.

In my opinion, at the national level to some extent there has been a shift in thinking and action and one can see that more minority ethnic people are being employed in Church House. However there is the perception that fair treatment may still be hindered by traditional attitudes, causing people to be stereotyped, excluded and not given proper consideration or fair treatment, especially with respect to training and promotional opportunities. It is important that all senior staff should undergo training in equal opportunities; this should not be considered optional. Currently EOP is included as an item on the staff appraisal forms. It is very important that the Archbishops' Council as the employer must be seen to be acting in a just manner.

With respect to the dioceses, it is my impression that for the most part dioceses appear to be content to say that they have a policy but there is no real commitment to implementing the policy, training staff and monitoring the policy. One still hears of suitable applicants not being appointed because the staff would not like it. And this is the Church!

Cognisance must be taken of the Race Relations (Amendment) Act 2000 and its implications, (note Appendix 11).

At the national level of the Church, the Appointments Committee has published 'Guidelines for Appointments to Church Decision – Making Bodies (2000–2005)' GS Misc. 621, with special reference. The Committee stated that the guidelines had been drawn up

> in order to guide its own work of making appointments to Boards, Councils, working parties, conferences etc. It also recommends them to others in the Church as an input – suitably adapted into their own processes of making decisions about such appointments.

A great deal of time was spent by Mr Christopher Ball in consultation and discussion with several persons in preparing that paper within his capacity as Secretary to the Appointments Committee.

Yet one has to wonder how seriously these matters are taken, for instance in the setting up of Working Parties, and delegates who are selected to represent the Church at national and international meetings. In 2001, Miss Vasantha Gnanadoss (GS member) voiced her concern about the Terms of Reference of a particular Working Party, which seemed to take no account of the multi-ethnic character of the Church of England. I would like to add that this is not an isolated case. Very occasionally, CMEAC was approached about possible names for service on various groups.

In conclusion, the Committee for Minority Ethnic Anglican Concerns has kept abreast of the progress of dioceses in Equal Opportunities with respect to the formulation and implementation of policies. Half the dioceses still do not have policies and in some instances where there is a policy it is not necessarily owned by the diocese. There are several dioceses with comprehensive policies, and they should be reviewed in the light of recent legislation. The development of an EOP within the structures has to be holistic, if it is to be effective. It requires thorough discussion and often a change of culture and behaviour in the way people are employed, nominated or elected to serve at all levels of the diocese.

The Church of England as the established Church must be seen to be fair in its recruitment, employment, training and promotion practices. People are increasingly becoming more aware of their rights so the Church must ensure that it is fully cognisant of the implications the Race Relations (Amendment) Act 2000, the Disability Discrimination Act, the Human Rights Act, as well as other legislation which impacts on Equal Opportunities. If not there will be the danger of the Church having to face the courts or settle out of court with large compensation packages. Yet overriding this ought to be a consciousness of the Church as the Body of Christ and the fundamental

Christian understanding that all human beings are created in the image of God, that all are valued equally by God and share equally in God's love.

All the hours spent preparing policies will come to nought if they are put on one side when decisions are to be made and it is business as usual through the old boys' network – *what people actually do in an organization tells what the organization really believes and values.*

chapter 17
Ethnic monitoring

Ethnic diversity poses questions about our ability to share together in a society based on justice and mutual respect. These are gospel questions which merit our focused attention, priority and urgency in the next few years.[1]

We need people from all walks of life and all backgrounds to be active in decision making.[2]

The fact that the GS was prepared to even discuss ethnic monitoring in 1999 was a big shift in its thinking when one remembers that in February 1989 members believed that the act of introducing ethnic monitoring and affirmative action into the Synod's electoral process was racist and discriminatory. The negative responses and non-responses given by some parish clergy to the survey of black Anglicans in 1993 as recounted earlier in this report signified a similar attitude. One of the decisions for the change of heart could well have been the publication of the Stephen Lawrence Inquiry Report (February 1999) and its impact on organizations.

The Diocese of Southwark, through the efforts of Ms Gnanadoss, the Revd Alan Gadd and others had pursued the matter of ethnic monitoring in the Battersea Deanery and then by 1997 through the Southwark Diocesan Synod.

The motion which was passed in the Diocesan Synod with a large majority read:

That this Synod:

a) recognise the advantages of showing that the Church of England is a multi-ethnic church with multi-ethnic leadership at all levels, and

b) calls upon the Archbishops' Council to organise the collection of statistics at the time of the next general revision of church electoral rolls (2002) on the ethnic origin of members on the electoral roll, members of church councils, church wardens, deanery synod representatives and clergy throughout all the dioceses of the Church of England.

In November 1999, the General Synod debated this motion which was approved with an additional proviso (that this Synod) … 'calls further upon the Archbishops' Council to arrange the collection of the statistics by the procedure suggested in the Background Paper from the Diocese of Southwark.'

As part of the 2002 Electoral Roll Revision, this exercise is being conducted by the Statistics Unit at the request of the General Synod. The ethnic categories which are being used are those employed by the Office for National Statistics in the 2001 UK Census. The findings will be reported to the General Synod in November 2002.

Initially, maybe due to someone's oversight, CMEAC was not consulted about the draft form and background notes for the dioceses. The Secretary was informed by a Diocesan Link Person that the dioceses had been sent information. The Secretary contacted the Statistics Unit, and a copy was sent to CMEAC's Secretary (24 September) and to CMEAC's Chairman (3 October), for reply by 8 October. Fortunately CMEAC was due to have its residential meeting shortly, so the draft was discussed by the Committee and a timely response was sent to the Statistics Unit. The Committee suggested that in connection with the responsibility to complete the form – the clause 'nevertheless you are under no obligation to complete the form' would send the wrong message and would give the wrong signals about the General Synod's commitment to the task.

Although there has been general approval, some dioceses have objected to this exercise, so the outcome is awaited. The support of the diocesan bishops is key to this process. The Diocese of Southwark has sent out posters and leaflets to all its churches and held briefing meetings for clergy and lay officers, in an effort to urge churchgoers to sign on the church electoral roll.

Leadership

We cling to a view of the Church with people like us keeping control of it. The trouble is that minority groups also see that view of the Church. They do not see a possibility of themselves sharing in that network of decision-making and control. They tell us that they feel their experience is the same when they come to church as it is when they go to work: they are tolerated up to a certain ratio, up to a certain level of responsibility but no more.[3]

… our ethnic origins may lie in Africa, the Americas, Asia or the Caribbean Islands, and a few of us are visitors from those lands, but mostly we ourselves are English ... we belong to this land and to every corner of it. Make us more visible within the life and leadership of our Church ...[4]

... contrast between the prophetic role and the continuing racism in some churches. Too often the organization of the churches' life merely reflects their social environment and members of society's weakest groups including the racially oppressed are also absent from leadership roles and the decision making process of the churches.[5]

In the Stephen Lawrence Inquiry November 2000 GS debate, in introducing the *Called to Lead* report, Dr Philip Giddings referred to the fact that

When we move from congregations as a whole to levels of participation in Church life, and particularly Church leadership, we see stark evidence of the way in which our attitudes, processes and behaviour are working to exclude black and Asian Anglicans. As the proportion of the minority ethnic population increases, there is a rising curve of participation as churchwardens, eucharistic assistants and sidespeople, but not for electoral rolls, deanery synods and clergy. In the Church of England, as in so many other institutions in our country, black and Asian people become less and less visible beyond a certain point in the structures. That simply should not be.

The Revd Simon Pothen in his address to the GS in November 2000 referred to the importance of mentoring of young minority ethnic clergy and ordinands which the Association of Black Clergy had been doing for over 30 years:

We live in a multi-ethnic, multi-cultural society, and the Church in all its structures must reflect that. I look around this body and there are not many black faces. I look at the House of Bishops and there are even fewer. I look at the Cathedral staff and there are even fewer. It is about manifesting that kind of visibility in all structures of the Church.

In the same debate, Bishop John Perry also called for the need for more role models locally.

In my opinion, the absence of role models is a serious form of impoverishment in the life of the Church. There needs to be a determined effort to appoint minority ethnic men and women to all levels of national, diocesan and local church organizations; at present there are approximately 200 minority ethnic clergy and yet there is a marked absence of minority ethnic clergy at a higher level than incumbent status. The Church needs to deliberately spot talent and work with persons with the potential to be promoted through training and positive support in the same way that other persons are identified, trained and supported. There is often the stereotypical assumption that the minority ethnic person is not up to the job – people need to be informed, equipped and supported in order to perform. Over the years CMEAC's work has been enriched by the diversity of its committee members and also the cultural and ethnic diversity of the Diocesan Network.

In our travels around the dioceses in inner city, urban, suburban and rural areas we were meeting capable minority ethnic people who were parishioners and wanted to contribute to the Church's ministry but they were being treated as though they were invisible by the Church. Yet some people were holding senior positions in various professions not only in dioceses such as London and Southwark but also in rural Lincoln, Norwich and York.

The Church of England has a wonderful gift – its diversity – it is important to value all people as individuals and treat them in ways which bring out the best in them. Over the centuries, the Church has shown its ability to work with other cultures overseas through its missionary societies. The challenge here is for the Church of England to embrace its cultural diversity, and work with and across cultures to create an environment in which people from all backgrounds can work together and be equally valued and affirmed to the building up of God's kingdom. The concept of valuing cultural diversity will only work if it is built into policies. In CMEAC, this is built into the Committee's Constitution, and permeates through its work.

> In the 1980s the Leicester Diocese took the bold step of making direct and specific constitutional provision for the representation of minority ethnic Anglicans on boards and councils ... it has brought more people from ethnic minorities into our decision making structures.[6]

The question must be asked: how is the Church of England managing and drawing on its cultural diversity? The question must also be asked to what extent are clergy in parishes encouraging leadership to emerge from majority ethnic, as well as minority ethnic parishioners? Institutional racism has denied minority ethnic Anglicans equality of opportunity, access and full participation in the church. It is time for the Church of England to make space for and really receive the gifts of minority ethnic Anglicans.

chapter 18

Valuing cultural diversity

... as one member of the project's group remarked, many of those in today's city police forces, who stand accused of institutional racism, may have begun their education in rural schools. In seeking to ensure that tragedies such as those experienced by the Lawrence family do not recur we must all recognise the need to celebrate cultural diversity in our rural schools and communities as no less urgent than it is in schools where cultural diversity is a visible presence and its positive effects more easily demonstrated. This is a collective responsibility of the whole church community. It cannot and should not be left to the teachers and those charged with directly supporting the Church of England's small rural schools.[1]

Inspectors are asked specifically to inspect for racism and to ask what action is being taken by schools to promote racial harmony, to prepare pupils for living in a diverse and increasingly interdependent society and specifically to address racism ... Inspectors are also expected to ask, does the school have strategies for promoting inclusion, including race equality and how well are they working?[2]

With respect to educating children and young people, the evidence given by Chief Constable Burden (South Wales Police) in the Stephen Lawrence Inquiry is relevant: ... racism exists within all organisations and institutions, and that it infiltrates the community and starts amongst the very young. Recent research in Cardiff showed that 50 per cent of the racist incidents considered by the Race Equality Council involved young people under 16 years old, and 25 per cent of these incidents involved children between the ages of 6 and 10 years. The problem is thus deeply ingrained. Radical thinking and sustained action are needed in order to tackle it head on, not just in the Police Service of our country, but in all organisations and in particular in the fields of education and family life.[3]

The *Valuing Cultural Diversity* project came about as a result of an Advisory Team visit to the Diocese of Hereford when Bishop Oliver spoke about the need for educational resources to address racism in rural schools. The team acknowledged that most of what was available was suited to inner city and urban areas but not really to rural areas. 'Racism in rural areas is expressed in different ways and different strategies are needed to fight it'[4]

In rural areas minority ethnic communities are small and scattered. They have no support, groups are isolated and lack a voice. Because they feel threatened and fear victimization people try to be invisible. During Advisory Team visits to rural dioceses, we met university students who were being racially abused, on as well as off the campus, as well as asylum seekers for whom that was a daily occurrence. I remember a colleague in Church House proudly showing me a poem which her son had written about a trapped animal. He was attending boarding school in a rural area, he was being racially abused and was trying to give his mother a message.

The *Valuing Cultural Diversity* Management Group was chaired by Mrs Gloria Rich, CMEAC member, and included Mr David Lankshear, Schools' Officer of the Board of Education and Deputy Secretary of the National Society; the Revd Jeremy Martineau, National Rural Officer; Mrs Glynne Gordon-Carter, CMEAC's Secretary; the Revd Prebendary Theo Samuel and Mrs Vinnette Melbourne, both of CMEAC, and Diocesan Directors of Education (DDEs) from the ten most rural dioceses. Other officers were invited as necessary, e.g. Mrs Diana Murrie, National Children's Officer, Board of Education. Initially the Management Group held a one-day consultation with the DDEs, in order to get their views. They fully supported the project as there was a great need for resources for rural primary schools.

The Management Group spent a great deal of time preparing the *Valuing Cultural Diversity* project and seeking funds from the dioceses, as well as the Central Church Fund. There was a good response from the advertisements for researchers as colleges and university departments of higher education wanted to be involved in the work. The research project was undertaken by Professor Maurice Galton, Homerton College, Cambridge and Dr Linda Hargreaves, University of Durham.

The specific terms of this pilot project set out:

- to establish what materials were currently available for work on cultural diversity in church primary schools in rural areas;
- to ascertain where teachers needed further assistance;
- to identify gaps in existing materials;

- to define and develop proposals for supporting and helping teachers either by the production of additional materials or in other ways.[5]

The researchers held face to face interviews with 43 headteachers from 6 of the most rural dioceses in England. The schools were chosen by diocesan officers to represent a range of practice. Three broad categories were identified:

- Schools with a low level of confidence and awareness (about 20 per cent of the sample).

- Schools that promoted cultural diversity mainly through multi-faith Religious Education (about two thirds of the sample).

- Schools which sought to give the whole curriculum a multi-cultural emphasis (about 16 per cent of the sample).[6]

The *Valuing Cultural Diversity in Rural Primary Schools* report was presented to the Management Group in Autumn 1999. It was a good quality document and offered a substantial amount of information on rural schools and how they were responding, as well as many practical recommendations for schools at different levels, and strategies which could be integrated into their programmes.

- For schools at the initial stage we suggest specific courses designed to improve confidence and competence in a multi-faith approach to the teaching of RE including the celebration of cultural diversity in those areas of the Literacy Hour and the National Curriculum where specific reference is made to multicultural activities within programmes of study.

- For schools which already offer a sound, well established multi-faith approach to RE we suggest an in-service programme designed to ensure that cultural diversity is celebrated across the whole curriculum, including anti-racist education, based upon clear policy statements. The programme should make use of case studies of existing good practice and also offer mentoring support through links with Diocesan advisers and other local teachers in schools where practice is more advanced.

- For schools which already offer a 'whole curriculum' approach, the in-service should concentrate on eliminating all aspects of 'institutional racism'. Staff should be helped to confront their own prejudices and with the support of a consultant be encouraged to reflect on ways on improving their own and colleagues' classroom practice.[7]

The report was discussed by the Archbishops' Council's Board of Education and meetings of education officers. The Management Group turned its attention to providing support for schools in the form of a Valuing Cultural Diversity Self-Evaluation Kit which the Board of Education would be putting out as resource material on their website.

This project was considered significant and appropriate not only because of the request from the Diocese of Hereford, as well as Truro, but also because the Church of England has nearly 5,000 church schools, of which a large number are rural primary schools. The report showed that in small village schools people were at different stages and needed the help of resource materials and staff development. There was well-documented evidence of racist attitudes in rural areas.

The report was given a lukewarm reception by the Board of Education and it was never given a proper profile as it was never published and never launched. This was extremely disappointing. CMEAC felt that where the Board considered issues had not been dealt with or had been overlooked, these could have been discussed. The researchers had provided well thought out and sound recommendations which were not being implemented. It almost felt as though 'the baby was being thrown out with the bath water'. A more positive approach to the report would have affirmed schools which were actively working and others would have felt that help and support was on the way. All schools need to regard the valuing of cultural diversity as central, and not peripheral, to the ethos of the school.

Yet the report was timely as it was presented in the same year that the Stephen Lawrence Inquiry Report was launched, and it did provide a response to that Report in the context of rural church schools. Some Diocesan Boards of Education (DBE) have responded positively to the report, e.g. the Bristol DBE had discussions with various headteachers and circulated a questionnaire on Valuing Cultural Diversity to its voluntary assisted schools. However, a strong endorsement of the report would have resulted in a much better response from most, if not all of the mainly rural dioceses. The Church of England has approximately 3,000 rural primary schools nationally and they have the potential to be agents of change in rural communities. The report can still be very useful in helping schools prepare for OFSTED Inspections which will be more rigorous in their approach (note quotation at the beginning of the chapter).

The *Valuing Cultural Diversity Report* identified the leadership which was necessary in order to help the schools to progress:

All initiatives designed to promote cultural diversity in rural church primary schools should be carefully co-ordinated and should be accompanied by a national launch involving parallel programmes of events at diocesan level. Preferably such programmes would involve teachers in the planning and be headed by a senior bishop who should also chair the proposed national forum ... the proposals set out will not cost vast sums of money. It is more a matter of providing information and support and harnessing the expertise that already exists to supply necessary training. More than anything it requires a demonstration by the leadership of the Church that it views the need for its rural schools to make the necessary changes to the curriculum as essential to its mission.[8]

The research had been funded with the help of the Central Church Fund and some of the dioceses. In the latter case, the Chairman of the Board of Education and the Chairman of CMEAC had written a joint letter to dioceses in order to inform them of the project and solicit their financial assistance. The report was meant to be Phase 1 of the *Valuing Cultural Diversity* project. The Board of Education's attitude to the report did not give much hope that finance would be forthcoming for Phase 2.

chapter 19

Support for majority ethnic clergy

... Parish clergy and those in other ministries should receive special training in racism awareness and cultural diversity as part of their post-ordination, in-service and lay training. Consideration should be given to providing a short course on these issues for clergy arriving in multi-cultural parishes for the first time.[1]

We need to ensure that effective resources for training and education in racism awareness and cultural diversity are in place and taken up, particularly by those in leadership positions, and that there are proper mechanisms to monitor and develop the quality of those resources and their effectiveness.[2]

It is perhaps easier to demonstrate one's opposition when faced with blatant examples among far right political parties or in the police or armed forces. It is harder to deal with such issues when they involve attitudes of indifference or complacency among members of one's own institution. The evidence of the headteachers (and we emphasise that we did not interview any clergy directly) is that there is more awareness of the problem inside school than inside the vicarage.[3]

I will recount four pieces of evidence in order to demonstrate the influence of parish clergy as the gatekeepers to the Church. Whether one has a good or bad experience in church is often influenced by the vicar's attitude and action.

CASE 1

Two parishioners were seeking a new spiritual home so they attended a nearby church. After worship the vicar welcomed the white woman and ignored the black woman and her daughter who were standing alongside. The woman and her daughter never returned to that church.

CASE 2

A priest telephones me from one of the rural parishes to report that an Asian family has moved in to run the local corner shop and their children are being harassed racially at school. He says that he is Chairman of the Board of Governors and does not know how to handle the situation as race issues were not part of his ordination training. He needs help.

CASE 3

A black worshipper approaches a stall to buy some books after church. She is quizzed about why she is attending that church instead of another which is nearer to her home by someone who is managing the stall. In the end she purchased no books and stopped going to church.

Several months passed and the vicar realized that she had stopped attending, yet she continued to send her offertory envelopes so he decided to visit her. She told him her story and eventually after a great deal of persuasion she returned to church.

CASE 4

A clergyman encourages a potential candidate to apply for a job advertised in the *Church Times* and even sends a copy of the advertisement to the person as the *Church Times* is not easily available. This woman decides to apply for the job and speaks to her vicar in order to get his advice in case she is short-listed. He suggests that she should read a particular church publication which he lends her and says he is willing to take her through 'a dry run' in preparation for the interviews. She is short-listed and is successful. I know because I was that person.

Without the support of David Jackson I would never have made it because I knew nothing about the Church at the national level and had not heard about *Faith in the City*. I also owe a debt of gratitude to Canon David Garlic who brought the advertisement to my attention and urged me to apply for the post – even to the extent of sending the advertisement.

Theological Colleges and Courses

The Committee has always written and spoken about the need for training in racism awareness to be included in the curricula for theological education. Clergy often speak of being ill-prepared for situations which arise and minority ethnic parishioners speak of clergy not knowing how to relate to them. Clergy play a significant role in parishes so it is critical for them to be aware of 'race' issues.

The Advisory Board of Ministry has been addressing these matters to some extent through the provision of an audit for use in colleges and courses. The audit was the work of the Initial Ministerial Education Committee, which expressed its expectations that the curricula would do the following:

- Include reference to cultural, ethnic and racial diversity within Christianity and within the Church of England, and treat this diversity as a reality to be valued.

- Emphasise that contemporary Britain is a multi-cultural, multi-racial and multi-religious society, and that many of its citizens experience pervasive prejudice and hostility, and both direct and indirect discrimination.

- Facilitate reflection on the role of individual Christians, and of the churches as institutions, in identifying, combating and reducing discrimination in modern society, and in building racial equality and justice.

- Promote cultural awareness of the ways in which churches and individual Christians sometimes fail to address issues of equality and justice, and on the contrary collude with inequality and injustice.[4]

Some insightful questions and suggestions are also given about matters of curriculum, organization and management. It is clear that the audit addresses racism both at the personal and institutional level.

In his presentation at the conference held by the Community Race Relations Unit of the British Council of Churches in 1992, the Revd Dr Brian Russell made reference to the audit. He said

The audit asks each college and course to appraise its educational programme, structures and management. It is not just a matter of managing or developing pastoral studies or mission studies in particular ways, but rather a matter of seeing the implications through the audit for the whole life, structure and educational programme of colleges and courses.

The audit is based on the assumption that there is a danger of subsuming issues of race under other important though related issues, such as concerns about the inner city or multi-faith. These kinds of concerns can help issues of race to be tackled but the *particularity* of issues of race also needs to be handled. For example, there is the need in supervising placements, whether these are in multi-ethnic communities or in hospitals or prisons, to help white ordinands to pick up the particular dimensions of race that may be hidden, though present.

The audit suggests that it is important that issues of race have a focus, as well as a permeation through the whole education programme. It is important for each college and course to consider what should be included in a focused handling of issues of 'race'. Examples might include how the history of Churches in post-war Britain is treated, or how aspects of theology is done and doctrine approached and communicated.[5]

The question needs to be asked whether and to what extent the audit has been used by theological colleges and courses?

By January 1998, ABM's paper entitled 'Beginning public ministry: Guidelines for ministerial formation and personal development for the first four years after ordination', under the heading of 'Expectations of initial and first-post training' listed training in racism awareness as one of the areas to which candidates should be exposed. The concern here is that training in racism awareness is considered as an expectation, it is not compulsory – therefore many students will opt out. Mrs Elizabeth Fisher in her speech at the General Synod debate on *The Passing Winter* (1996) drew reference to the fact that such training was compulsory for Methodist candidates. The Revd Charles Lawrence, Chairman CMEAC's Vocations Sub-Committee acknowledges that

the Church of England is finding ways to make appropriate responses to racism within its structures. It seems clear that addressing racism through ordination training is a major part of the answer. Such a 'bottom-up' approach might take some time to show results, but is probably the most effective long-term strategy.[6]

In his Draft Agenda for Action, Bishop John Sentamu stated that with respect to theological colleges and courses, training in racism awareness and valuing cultural diversity need to be further encouraged in the programmes of theological colleges and courses. The findings of inspectors need to be monitored by the Inspectors Working Party. With respect to the monitoring of such training, maybe more needs to be done in terms of inspections.

All theological colleges and courses should consider training in these matters as a requirement, without which ordinands will be ill prepared as leaders in community, given the multi-ethnic, multi-cultural and multi-faith nature of British society.

Part 6

The Stephen Lawrence Inquiry Report

chapter 20

The Church of England's response to the Stephen Lawrence Inquiry Report

It is incumbent upon every institution to examine their policies and the outcome of their policies and practices to guard against disadvantage in any section of our communities.[1]

The Archbishops' Council is very conscious of two things. The first is that words are not enough; it is action that is needed, action which has a demonstrable, visible effect upon our Church life. The second is that there are no quick fixes which will achieve that; we cannot remedy in months something which is the product of centuries of injustice ... What we are engaged upon is a process of achieving deep-seated change, change within ourselves as well as within our Church.[2]

I am fully aware of my pain and I am not ignorant of the tension that some of you feel at having to confront the issues of racism, but as long as you keep trying to avoid it or denying it we cannot work together to eradicate it and to go forward as children of God.[3]

It is very important, indeed essential – that racial awareness training takes place in the rural dioceses to uncover the racism which is often disguised behind a kind paternalism, behind the niceness which means that we do not see a person as a person but as a type, not seeming to care about their individuality, their history and their culture.[4]

The Stephen Lawrence Inquiry Report

On 22 April 1993, Stephen Lawrence (aged 18 years) was murdered by five white youths in an unprovoked racist attack while waiting for a bus in Eltham. The fact that no one was condemned for Stephen's murder and the unprofessional manner in which the tragedy was handled by the police, led Mr and Mrs Lawrence to campaign for justice. By July 1997, the Home Secretary met with them and agreed that there should be a Public Inquiry 'to inquire into the matters arising from the death of Stephen Lawrence on 22nd April 1993 to date, in order particularly to identify the lessons to be learned for the investigation and prosecution of racially motivated crimes'. Sir William MacPherson conducted the Inquiry; the Rt Revd Dr John Sentamu, the Bishop of Stepney and Chairman of CMEAC, served as a member of the team.

The report made 70 recommendations: 66 related to the police service, the remaining 4 recommendations concerned strategies to prevent and address racism through education. The final recommendation called on police services, local government and other relevant agencies specifically to 'consider implementing community and local initiatives aimed at promoting cultural diversity and addressing racism and the need for focused consistent support for such initiatives'.

The report defined racism and institutional racism and stated that it did not regard either form of racism as particular to the police.

The Hon. Jack Straw, Home Secretary, presented the Stephen Lawrence Inquiry Report to Parliament on 24 February 1999. The print and electronic media gave many column inches, as well as air time discussing different aspects of the report and getting the reactions of key people such as the police, the Lawrence family, the Inquiry Team, legal representatives, and the public. The report was of immense importance and was seen as the most significant race relations report since the Scarman report on the Brixton riots in April 1981.

I assumed that the Church of England as the established Church would give the report a high profile in terms of how the Church as an institution should respond. Bishop John Sentamu had been a member of the Inquiry Team and his knowledge could be of great value in advising the Church. Initially, the Committee was not consulted and when I raised the question as to whether Bishop John would be invited to address the General Synod in July 1999, I was informed that it was possible that he could address a 'fringe' meeting. It seemed as though the report would be treated as a 'fringe' report and CMEAC as a 'fringe' Committee, as well-meaning people started planning in a flurry how the Church should respond, without consulting with CMEAC. Yet this was the Committee mandated to work with the Church to combat institutional racism, and had been doing so in a very significant way since 1987. At this stage I wrote to the Secretary General and gave reasons why the Stephen Lawrence Inquiry Report should be given a proper profile on the forthcoming General Synod agenda, the importance of having Bishop John Sentamu address the General Synod, as well as the necessity for the

Archbishops' Council to discuss with CMEAC about how the Church should respond to the report.

The situation was retrieved and CMEAC was consulted. The Committee decided that the Archbishops' Council should be advised by Bishop John. He was invited to present a paper to the Archbishops' Council and they in turn asked him to present it to the House of Bishops. Also space was made on the General Synod's agenda in July 1999 for Bishop John to present his paper, followed by some discussion. Mr Neville Lawrence, Stephen's father, was invited to attend the session.[5] He was welcomed by the Archbishop of Canterbury and was given a standing ovation. The Archbishop thanked Bishop John for his contribution and then gave his own reflections. He said that the Church must move beyond gestures – a radical change of heart, genuine repentance which we as Christians know, was required. 'We cannot afford to rest, either as a Church or as a society, until we have confronted racism at its deepest level, in ourselves, in our nation, in the structures of the Church, in the ordained ministry and in congregational life.'

Bishop John's paper on the Stephen Lawrence Inquiry Report and how the Church should respond was very well received by General Synod. His draft agenda for action for the Church of England contained two main strands for the Church of England to address in response to the Stephen Lawrence Inquiry Report. The report suggested that there should be an agenda for external action which should relate to support for the police, and victims and witness support.

The Agenda for action internally (i.e. within the Church) highlighted the importance of the following:

1. Resources and training in Racism Awareness and Valuing Cultural Diversity.
2. Prevention and the role of education in Church schools and colleges.
3. Monitoring of the Agenda for Action.
4. Definitions.
5. Publications and communications.
6. Racist language.
7. Theological colleges and courses.
8. Local churches.
9. Archbishops' priority.

In addressing the General Synod, Bishop John Sentamu called on the Church both to play a part in implementing its recommendations and to 'put our own house in order'. Replying on behalf of the Council, Dr Philip Giddings promised that the Council, 'building and extending the work that is already in train, will draw together an action plan which co-ordinates and prioritises what is to be done'. The General Synod had taken Bishop John Sentamu's paper seriously and the Archbishops' Council, with the guidance of a multi-disciplinary staff team led by Mr Richard Hopgood, Director of Policy, together with representatives from BSR, the Ministry Division, Board of Education, the Board of Mission, the Communications Unit, Statistics Unit and CMEAC, would set out strategies for consideration by the Council.

By November 1999, the GS received from the Archbishops' Council a report on initiatives which were being carried out.

Follow-up Action Plan – National Level

The first stage of the action plan had the following elements:

1. Initiatives to help implement the recommendations of the Inquiry's report with reference to the police, etc.

2. Educational initiatives and resources to help schools and church groups address and embrace cultural diversity.

3. A statistical exercise to gather figures from (say) six dioceses to determine how minority ethnic people are represented in the life of the Church – so that we can see what has changed since *How We Stand* (1994); and so that we have a secure statistical base from which to set future targets and objectives.

4. Listening to minority ethnic people both through existing networks and recent surveys and through focus groups to hear what they are saying and feeling about the Church and what they wish to see changed.

5. A commitment – starting with the Archbishops' Council – to experimental learning about racism to engender a new sense of shared understanding and urgency.

One year later by November 2000, the Archbishops' Council presented a follow up report to the General Synod entitled *Called to Lead: A Challenge to Include Minority Ethnic People*. The report had been prepared by the Stephen Lawrence Follow-up Staff Group.

The main purpose of the 2000 report was to identify the progress which had been in each of the action areas as agreed by the Archbishops' Council in 1999 as well as to set out the programme for the second phase. *Called to Lead* was well-received by the GS which asked that all members should commit themselves to race awareness training. Already the Archbishops' Council was setting an example as some members had been trained.

The following General Synod motion was put and carried:

> That this Synod encourage the Archbishops' Council to pursue the second stage of the action plan set out in GS Misc. 625 and to report back to the Synod on progress.

The Stephen Lawrence Inquiry Report acted as a catalyst and forced the Church to take a fresh look at itself with respect to its record in combating institutional racism.

In his Presidential Address to Southwark Diocesan Synod on 13 March 1999, Bishop Tom Butler referred to the Stephen Lawrence Inquiry Report as a 'kairos' moment, a moment when history shakes and new possibilities open. With respect to the dioceses, approximately one third had launched specific initiatives to address the Stephen Lawrence Inquiry Report by 2000. I would expect that with the publication of CMEAC's *Good Practice Paper for Dioceses* in 2001 more dioceses have been responding. The Diocese of Southwark was the first to respond to the report. In September 1999, the bishops of the diocese commissioned a three-person team to conduct an independent enquiry into racism within the structures of the Diocese of Southwark. This was, of course, a very brave move because with the report would come recommendations and one wondered whether the diocese would really act on the recommendations? The history of this work in the Church will show that Southwark Diocese has always been a leader – the first to appoint a minority ethnic bishop, Bishop Wilfred Wood, the only diocese to have had a Race Relations Commission, the only diocese with a Black Anglican Forum and the second diocese to have formulated an Equal Opportunities Policy, Birmingham being the first.

The Terms of Reference for the Southwark review were as follows:

1. to review the current policies, procedures, practices and structures against legal requirements and best race equality practice and to make recommendations to the Bishop of Southwark for consideration and implementation;
2. to produce a report of the Inquiry.

The Inquiry Panel consisted of Sir Herman Ouseley, now Lord Ouseley, at that time he was Chairman of the Commission for Racial Equality; Mrs Glynne Gordon-Carter, Secretary to the Archbishops' Council's Committee for Minority Ethnic Anglican Concerns and the Revd David Haslam, former Secretary of the Churches' Commission for Racial Justice. A back-up team consisting of Messers Paul Buxton, Andrew Lane from the diocese, and Mr Paul Riddell from the CRE supported the panel. In the Foreword to the report, Lord Ouseley said

> In effect the Diocese of Southwark has sought an audit of its achievements and performance to date. By having its processes and practices scrutinised it has invited suggestions for improving its record on equality and achieving its objective of maximising participation by all sections of the community in the work of the church, at parish, deanery and diocesan levels.[6]

The Diocese of Southwark received the report in February 2000 and debated it at their Diocesan Synod in July.

The Rt Revd Dr Tom Butler, Bishop of Southwark, has expressed a personal commitment to, and responsibility for, whatever changes are required. Subsequently the diocese has been carrying out a number of initiatives:

1. the Equal Opportunities Committee had been formed;

2. the Diocesan Committee for Minority Ethnic Anglican Concerns has been formed and officers appointed: Mr Delbert Sandiford, the Executive Officer, with an Administrative Officer;

3. selection and appointment patterns for minority ethnic ordinands and clergy were receiving attention;

4. the Boards of Education and Church in Society had produced action plans for taking forward the recommendations in the report which were particularly relevant to them – the Diocesan CMEAC had received those plans;

5. the bishop's staff meeting had received 'Race' Awareness Training and that would also be held for members of the Bishop's Council.

I would hope that, two years later, a great deal more has been done.

With respect to other dioceses, and their response to the Stephen Lawrence Inquiry Report, the Bishop of Birmingham commissioned an independent report into the diocese's practices and the Diocese of Bradford was also conducting a review. In several dioceses the bishop's staff have undergone racism awareness training, for example: Blackburn, Chester, Gloucester, Guildford, Oxford, Portsmouth, Sheffield, Manchester and York. As mentioned earlier, the Archbishops' Council was setting an example by itself undergoing racism awareness training. It is commendable that several dioceses are undertaking racism awareness training at the senior levels but I hope that it is not just a case of 'that is it, we have had training'. The next step must be 'How can we use our training to address the issues that have been raised in the Stephen Lawrence Inquiry Report, as well as the CMEAC reports? How can we encourage others who hold key positions in the diocese to have this training?' *Called to Lead: A Challenge to Include Minority Ethnic People* provides for the Church substantial and vital information which dioceses should be discussing with a view to action.

chapter 21
A different reality?

Why do you look at me like that?
With all that hate and fear in your heart?
But you are wrong.
You are thinking the thoughts of generations before you.
You are unaware of this.
And we suffer for it.[1]

I think the only difference between the people on the Windrush and our children is this, we came asking for our rights, they are going to demand them.[2]

Black and white people, as the writer Salman Rushdie remarked some years ago, inhabit different worlds – it is black people who suffer the degradations, the injustices and the threats to their security of the immigration control system. They who are required to produce their passports to establish their immigration status and the legality of their presence here when they claim benefits or seek services. They who are attacked in their homes, schools and public places because of their physical appearance. They who are regarded by people in authority, and portrayed in the press, as an alien threat from which the rest of society must be defended. This is the reality of racism in Britain in the late 1980s, a reality which contradicts any rhetoric of equality or equal opportunities.[3]

The above comment is just as relevant at the beginning of the twenty-first century, as in the late 1980s. Gordon spoke about a deepening of the division in British society along the lines of 'race' and skin colour in the 1980s. He argued that minority ethnic groups continue to experience a different reality.

Minority ethnic communities are contributing in very positive ways to British society and despite racial discrimination some have progressed and achieved success. However what also must be set alongside that is the reality of day to day living for many minority ethnic people: high unemployment, low wages, and housing shortages which disproportionately affect minority ethnic people.

It is estimated that between 1993–4, 20,000 people were racially attacked, 40,000 were subjected to racially motivated property damage and 230,000 were racially abused or insulted ... Overall then the survey results would suggest that over a quarter of a million people were subjected to some form of racial harassment in a twelve-month period.[4]

Between 1994/1995 and 1997/1998 African-Caribbean pupils were over four to six times more likely to be excluded than white pupils, although they were not more likely to truant than others, and many of those who were excluded tended to be higher or average ability, although the school saw them as underachieving.[5]

There is also an increase in exclusion of Bangladeshi, Pakistani and Somali pupils. With respect to exclusions, at the GS debate on *The Passing Winter*, Mrs Beverley Ruddock (Oxford) referred to the alarming rate of increase in the number of children and young people excluded from schools, including church schools. Mrs Ruddock said

This is substantiated by recently published research findings, including those of OFSTED, The Runnymede Trust, Dr Maude Blair of the Open University, the Commission for Racial Equality. A mounting body of empirical evidence shows that African-Caribbean pupils of both sexes suffer disproportionate levels of permanent exclusions from school. They are up to six times more likely to be permanently excluded than pupils from any other ethnic group. David Gilborne states that in some areas it is no exaggeration to say that the exclusion of black pupils has reached crisis point ... Dr Parsons has described permanent exclusion from school as 'officially sanctioned neglect'.

Research done by the Commission on the *Future of Multi-Ethnic Britain* stated that

questionnaires filled in by three quarters of all black and Asian participants agreed with the statement that in Britain, much racism is subtle and hidden. Four fifths agreed that many people pretend not to be racist but are. It is also the case that subtle and hidden forms of racism are draining and depressing, particularly when institutionalised in the structures and cultures of public bodies.[6]

Many refugees and asylum-seekers in Britain, as well as in other parts of Europe experience (on a daily basis) verbal abuse and physical violence. Minority ethnic young people feel particularly disadvantaged, they are often singled out by the police and targeted by right-wing groups. There have been a number of brutal assaults, namely: Rohit Duggal, a school boy stabbed and killed in Eltham, south-east London; Stephen Lawrence, an 18-year-old stabbed to death while waiting for a bus in the same area; also Shiji Lapite who died in police custody. 'Between 1992 and 1994, 15 people died in Britain as a result of what are believed to be racially motivated attacks' (CARF 1991–95). It is noticeable that a number of black people have died in police custody over the years. The Churches' Commission for Racial Justice on behalf of the churches has written articles, made representation to the government and campaigned about this issue.

The 'Future of multi-ethnic Britain' report reminds us that the Windrush celebrations represented the good side of multiculturalism. The Stephen Lawrence Inquiry Report with its disturbing finding of institutional racism in the police service, and by extension in all public bodies and institutions, was a sombre reminder of the challenges that must be faced.

Part 7

Review and looking towards the future

chapter 22

CMEAC'S relationship with the structures

Recognizing that the new structures would bring about changes and in order to ensure that the Committee continued to be at the centre, before Bishop John Sentamu stepped down as Chairman in 1999 he ensured that certain matters were sorted out. The first was the Committee's relationship to the Archbishops' Council, its accountability to the Council; the second was its constitution. Bishop John Sentamu provided the strong leadership which was needed at a critical point in its development. Restructuring was taking place at the national level as a result of the Turnbull Report.

The *Faith in the City* report was quite specific that in combating racism a clear lead should be given from the centre. The Committee has remained true to its mandate and is very much encouraged by the response from the Archbishops' Council to the Stephen Lawrence Inquiry Report.

The Archbishops' Council

The Archbishops' Council was set up in January 1999 as a result of the restructuring brought about by the Turnbull Report. By July 1999, the Council had set out its vision, purpose and values. Under Theme One 'Engaging with Social Issues', item b) stated: 'to enable the Church to understand and confront the reality of racism both in society and its own life'.

> In implementing the action plan drawn up in response to the Report of the Stephen Lawrence Enquiry and other related work, we will:
>
> - undertake appropriate training to raise our own awareness of racism in Church and society (both urban and rural);
> - develop the next stage of an action plan in response to the Stephen Lawrence Enquiry; [1]
> - support the work of the Board for Social Responsibility on the experience of minority ethnic people in the justice and penal systems

(thus following up the General Synod's Debate on prisons in November '99);

- monitor the work of the Church with refugees and asylum seekers following the passage of the Immigration and Asylum Act;

- review the Church's current commitment to racial justice work and education through the Committee for Minority Ethnic Anglican Concerns,, the Church and World Division, the Division of Ministry and the Churches' Commission for Racial Justice, and the opportunities for further ecumenical engagement in this area.[2]

a) Accountability

Within the new structures CMEAC would be directly accountable to the Archbishops' Council. This meant that the Committee's minutes and reports would be sent to the Council and the papers of the Archbishops' Council would be sent to CMEAC's Chairman and Secretary. Major pieces of work would have to be approved by the Council. The Committee was very pleased to welcome the Revd Canon Hugh Wilcox, Prolocutor, as the Archbishops' Council's representative on CMEAC.

The Stephen Lawrence Inquiry Report had given renewed impetus to the work and CMEAC was very pleased at the declaration which the Archbishops' Council had made about its commitment to racial justice and education about the issues. Yet the Church has to go further than making statements if institutional racism is to be eradicated.

The Committee's constitution and membership

With respect to its membership under the new structures, the Committee would still have representatives from boards and councils. Given the Appointments Committee's role in the structures it was important to have a representative from that committee as a member of CMEAC, and that was granted. The Committee welcomed Mrs Christina Rees as a representative from the Appointments Committee. Ms Jayne Ozanne has since replaced Mrs Rees.

Instead of allocating six places to House of Bishops' nominees (they were usually nominated from the Diocesan Network by CMEAC's Chairman), five places should be allocated accordingly, and one place would be given to the House of Bishops so that a representative from that body would serve on CMEAC. The other categories of membership would continue to exist. The Archbishops' Council gave their approval to the changes in CMEAC's membership.

The Committee's methodology

The Committee has had a busy agenda since its inception in 1987. In keeping with its Terms of Reference its focus has been to work within the structures at the national level, as well as with the dioceses.

The Committee's place within the structures, its accountability to the Archbishops' Council, its Terms of Reference and the support which is given by the House of Bishops has meant that CMEAC is taken seriously by the church structures. These key aspects are strengths of CMEAC's work. The Committee's monitoring role is also another strong element of its work.

CMEAC has implemented its programme of work through a range of strategies namely: the conduct of surveys in order to establish its credibility, monitoring, advocacy, supporting and resourcing work and developing educational resources. Appendices 15 and 16 provide lists of CMEAC members from 1996–2001 and 2001–2005.

During the first five years of the Committee's work meetings were held five or six times per year including one annual residential meeting. Currently the Committee meets three times per year (one meeting is residential).

Within recent years, due to the expansion of work, the approach has been to set up specialist sub-Committees to carry forward specific areas of work. Information and recommendations from those sub-Committees are reported regularly to CMEAC for decision.

The setting up of sub-Committees has meant that the Committee can co-opt persons to serve from the CMEAC Diocesan Network as well as Committee members with the appropriate background/interest. This style of working has meant that on completion of a particular project, the respective sub-Committee is terminated. It is important to ensure that each sub-Committee has strong links with CMEAC, therefore committee members serve on each of the sub-Committees – and usually chair those groups. It is important to ensure that in considering membership there is a balance in terms of ethnicity, lay and clergy and gender participation.[3]

Resources

With respect to the proposed Commission on Black Anglican Concerns, *Faith in the City* had proposed in relation to staffing:

a) one full-time staff officer based in the General Synod Office on a fixed-term contract as Secretary of the new Commission.

b) a full-time worker in BSR, funded by the Synod and responsible to that Board, but reporting also to the Commission;

c) a Selection Secretary in ACCM with responsibilities for black Anglican vocations, who would be responsible to the ACCM Council (to which a senior black clergyman would be nominated by the House of Bishops) but who would report also to the new Commission.

The FITC report expected that those posts would be filled by black Anglicans. Although it might be unlawful for them to be advertised to be filled by black people per se, the relevant job description would need to call for candidates to have a good knowledge of the minority ethnic communities, and the particular concerns of black Anglicans. Lay people would clearly be eligible, as well as suitably qualified clergy.[4]

With respect to item c) a Selection Secretary was appointed in course of time – Mrs Margaret Sentamu. Her responsibilities were as other Selection Secretaries and not specific to black Anglican vocations. In 2001, Mrs Sentamu was interviewed and subsequently promoted to the post of Senior Selection Secretary. The Revd Canon Dr John Sentamu, in response to the recommendations, was invited to serve on the ACCM Council.

Concerning item b) a full-time worker was appointed initially in 1987. By June 1990 the RCRC learnt that the request from CBAC for a full-time officer had been agreed in principle by the Policy Sub-Committee. This was to be achieved within the existing cash limit. This meant that the officer would be transferred to CBAC (BSR's 1990 Annual Report). The Board for Social Responsibility reluctantly accepted that decision. Mr David Skidmore, Board Secretary, was asked to seek interim funding so that the RCRC's work could continue. Eventually the RCRC post was reinstated as a part-time position. Eventually this work became part of the responsibility of BSR's officer for Community and Urban Affairs. I felt that was not a good decision mainly because it would send the wrong message that 'race' was an urban issue. It remains to be seen whether the Guildford Review, which is looking at structures at the national level, recommends otherwise in 2002.

It should be stated that prior to the decision to transfer me to CBAC, by November 1988 BSR's Executive Committee had recognized that I needed assistance because of having to divide my time between the work of RCRC and CBAC. The BSR's Secretary (Prebendary John Gladwin) had met with the Chairman of CBAC, the Chairman of RCRC and the Secretary in order to discuss the future needs of both Committees.

> We all agreed that there is too much work for Glynne to undertake alone. We further agreed that we need to look for a colleague for her. The view expressed yesterday was that we needed to seek someone of skill and that this would mean an SEO graded post. That would require Glynne's post to be regraded to Principal level.[5]

In an interview with Bishop John Sentamu related to the writing of this report as the person who had chaired the Committee the longest, he expressed his disappointment that I had never been appointed a Principal Officer and had never been given a proper level of staff support. He said that from the beginning the financial situation was not properly resolved and financial implications had not followed decisions. The Committee's Terms of Reference were never considered in the light of the financial implications. Bishop John felt that the greatest failure of the Church was to give people pieces of work without working out in management terms what that meant. Bishop Wilfred Wood, the first Chairman of the Committee had said at the time of my recruitment that the post should be graded at the Principal Officer level.

Throughout my fourteen years work for the Committee, the under-resourcing of the work was never resolved and yet with proper staffing levels so much more could have been achieved. As the officer in charge of developing the work I was aware on a daily basis that I could not advance the work in accordance with my vision, due to the lack of a proper level of assistance.

1. With respect to the youth work we had raised expectations which we could not fulfil because there was not the staff to undertake that area of work on an 'ongoing' basis. For a while I was able to get assistance from a volunteer who did a great deal to highlight and develop that programme but after she left the work went on the 'back burner'.
2. It was difficult to do the necessary monitoring after diocesan visits with respect to the implementation of recommendations we had made.
3. The 1994 Black Anglican Celebration brought to the fore new issues, a wider agenda. Again this highlighted the need for additional staff.
4. With each revision of the Committee's Terms of Reference in 1990 and 1996 there was an expansion of work, and staff resources were not taken into account.

5. The success of the work raised other expectations from within the Church of England, as well as other denominations, and that meant additional assignments.

6. The complexity, diversity and volume of the work were obvious, yet I was never provided with an assistant who could have undertaken certain areas of the work.

7. My role as secretary to the Committee was advisory, administrative, as well as developmental; the job description is attached as Appendix 12. In order to fulfil some aspects of the Committee's work I had to raise funds through the presentation of project proposals, as CMEAC's budget was extremely limited.

8. Eventually the pressure of work meant that I had to take the difficult decision to resign from serving on some agencies involved in working with black majority churches, namely the Black Christian Concerns Group of the Churches Together in England, the African Caribbean Evangelical Alliance (ACEA) and the Centre for Black and White Christian Partnership.

Some years ago a training consultant was brought in to assess training needs in Church House. At our interview her opening sentence was, 'I have been reading the Committee's publications – you operate like a Board but where is your staff?' My counterparts in the other denominations, e.g. the Methodists and the Roman Catholics, were properly resourced and supported. The need for a good level of administrative support was never recognized and never taken seriously. I am hoping that my remarks do not fall on deaf ears and that my successor will have adequate staff support, as the job has as one of its components visits to dioceses which requires the person to be away from the office on very many occasions. An assistant is needed at the level of an executive officer as the job encompasses the national level and the dioceses; it is an onerous responsibility.

Under paragraph 12.3 of the paper entitled *Towards an Agenda for Action for the Church of England* (1999), Bishop John stated that CMEAC has a monitoring role. It cannot adequately do its work with one full-time Secretary. The Church of England needs to face up to the challenge of monitoring the work in racism awareness, training and valuing cultural diversity. CMEAC hopes to publish examples of good practice from all the dioceses of the Church of England. Somebody needs to monitor it.

I found it extremely difficult to accept the excuse of cash limitations when from time to time all around I observed the increase in staff in other departments and the apparent ease with which some promotions were made. With respect to CMEAC it appeared that the Church was saying, 'This is as far as we intend to go with financing this work.' In looking through the records, it appears that the Church of England has never considered this work as one of its priorities, so it has been consistently under resourced.

The Revd Barney Pityana spoke about the lack of adequate resources for the Revd Ken Leech thus:

> I found Ken Leech's reflections on his task in his job as the staff officer for the Race, Pluralism and Community Group of the Board for Social Responsibility very consuming. I have to say to him though, I do not envy him. He does have a very difficult job on his hands. I am left with two impressions. First that one person is expected to do a job of such magnitude with limited resources and a skeleton staff ...[6]

Canon Smith-Cameron in his address to the General Synod regarding the establishment of the Committee for Black Anglican Concerns spoke about the fact that

> ACUPA had asked for three black posts. We are now conceded one or perhaps one and a bit, and that one to cover a mammoth task ... it is asking an awful lot for one person to do both his job (meaning the Revd Ken Leech) and to service the new proposed committee. It may prove a sure recipe to ensure the failure of getting the work of this committee off the ground. I trust that if we accept the suggestion put before us will recognise that what is being offered is but a small morsel towards what is really required for this task to be creatively engaged in.[7]

I am very pleased to note that the officer whom the Southwark Diocese has appointed to do the work of their Committee for Minority Ethnic Anglican Concerns has been employed at a proper level commensurate with his responsibilities, and he is being provided with an assistant at an appropriate level.

Reflections on work at Church House, Westminster

When I was employed in December 1987 I was told that I was the first black person to be employed in a senior post – Senior Executive Officer. I realized that in a way this meant that there were certain expectations – expectations which the organization had of me, expectations which the black community had, and expectations which I had of myself. So early on I decided that I would just be myself and act in a professional manner. As a trained teacher, headmistress of an Anglican Secondary School in Trinidad, Executive Director of the Family Planning Association of Trinidad and Tobago, and teacher at Bacon's School in London (Church secondary), I had a great deal of experience and training on how to relate to people and to do my work professionally. I felt that I was therefore well-equipped in how to work in this new situation.

I remember going into the lift on my first morning and a member of staff said hello and asked if I was new secretarial staff, as in those days no black person held any senior position. I explained that I wasn't but that I was looking for a secretary. When I started working in Church House every black person who came to the reception was directed to my office whether or not they had concern with my committee's work.

In the early days, especially, it was usual for me to be the only black person and maybe the only woman at meetings. It was not unusual to find that the minutes of a meeting would either not minute a significant point which I had made or it would be minuted as someone else's contribution. Sometimes CMEAC was told that a particular report should be reviewed by this or that board/council, yet some boards/councils wrote reports which included matters of concern to CMEAC, which was not consulted.

For one reason or another I had to move office eight times in fourteen years and the main reason was that some other section wanted space. The existing CMEAC office is isolated from the rest of the Secretariat of which it is supposed to be a part – the nearest neighbour is the Crockford Office with which we haven't the remotest connection.

As the officer responsible for developing the work of the Committee for Minority Ethnic Anglican Concerns (the former CBAC), I had to lift the profile of the work and earn the respect of colleagues on a professional level. This meant understanding the culture and ethos of the Church; being on time and prepared for meetings; dressing appropriately; learning the language of diplomacy; being able to work with colleagues on projects for the furtherance of the work; learning to write in a style acceptable to the Church; and holding my point without being perceived as aggressive. Working in the field of race relations is never easy, especially working for the Church – that had special challenges. I think that I was able to survive because of my belief in the work, belief in myself, and belief in God who guided and inspired me to do his work.

It would be remiss of me not to comment on the chairmanship of the Committee by Bishop John Sentamu. He provided the kind of leadership that the Committee needed to see it through some difficult issues. These included the Committee's redesignation and restructuring at Church House. The Committee was also called on to give its views on issues such as the Synodical Review, the Turnbull Commission and the Clergy Conditions of Service. Bishop John also took CMEAC through some memorable events such as *The Passing Winter* debate, the 1994 Black Anglican Celebration for the Decade of Evangelism, and the 1998 and 1999 Vocations Conferences. From time to time as he was able, Bishop John accompanied us on diocesan advisory team visits. The Committee grew from strength to strength under his leadership. During this period, CMEAC became more involved in ecumenical work. In fact, the Chairman assisted with the preparation of the worship material, especially the Bible reflections for the chosen lesson for the first Racial Justice Sunday Pack (1995), organized by the Churches' Commission for Racial Justice. Some prayers from the Committee's pre-Celebration pack were used. Despite his busy schedule, Bishop John always found time for CMEAC's work and so I felt well supported. He made an enormous contribution to the development of the Committee.

chapter 23

Future 'Seeds of Hope'?

I am very encouraged by the ways in which, increasingly, black people are holding positions of leadership within our Church both as clergy and laity. But I am also aware that there is still much to be done. I long for the day when every member of our Church will have the freedom to exercise the God-given abilities they possess.[1]

I ask again, have we who are called white really taken into account that it is we who are the minority ethnic community of world Christianity, that the time is now or very soon when Christianity will mostly be African, and when Europeans and Americans simply cannot expect to continue to prescribe its shape and character? Can we be content till we have a ministry as varied in ethnic and cultural background as the communities and congregations of our diocese? Can we accept that long after we have ceased even to remember what the debate about the ordination of women was about (and you know the passion I bring to that issue), we shall still be ordaining hardly any of our black members?[2]

We need to go and look at all the ways in which we do things and ask questions about what we are doing, whether we are excluding and discouraging part of our membership.[3]

The title of this section reminds the reader that *Seeds of Hope* was a seminal report in the work of the Committee and the mission and ministry of the Church. *Seeds of Hope* was launched in 1991 and so it is appropriate to use that report as a yardstick to measure what progress has been made by the church ten years on.

The national level

1. The Archbishops' Council is leading the way in responding to the Stephen Lawrence Inquiry Report, as well as to the concerns which minority ethnic Anglicans have always expressed through CMEAC. Bishop John Sentamu's draft *Agenda for the Church of England*, which was written as the Church's response to the Stephen Lawrence Inquiry Report, has helped to focus the thinking of the Archbishops' Council.

2. The Archbishops' Council is committed to the work and that is clearly stated in the Council's themes for the 2000–2005 quinqennium.

3. On the whole the General Synod's boards and councils have been responding positively, and collaborating with CMEAC as necessary.

4. Members of the General Synod are much more aware of the issues and they have acknowledged the need for the Church to combat institutional racism. This was evident in the debates on *The Passing Winter: A Sequel to Seeds of Hope* (1996) and the *Called to Lead* report (2000). Some members have had training in racism awareness, others have committed themselves to having training during this quinquennium. At the debate on *Called to Lead* a straw poll was taken which revealed that 158 members had been trained.

5. The Committee's monitoring is taken seriously by the structures at the national and diocesan levels.

6. Minority ethnic Anglicans are slowly becoming more visible in the life of the Church at the national level. The following appointments have been made since the Committee's existence: the Revd Dr Herman Browne, Anglican Communion Adviser to the Archbishop of Canterbury; the Revd Canon Smith-Cameron, a Royal Chaplain to the Queen; the Revd Canon Dr John Sentamu, the first minority ethnic person to be appointed Prolocutor of the Province of Canterbury (he was re-elected in 1996 unopposed) and was later appointed Bishop of Stepney; the Revd Theo Samuel made Prebendary of St Paul's Cathedral; Bishop Michael Nazir-Ali, Bishop of Rochester; and Bishop John Sentamu recently appointed Bishop of Birmingham. In Church House, Mrs Margaret Sentamu has been appointed to the post of Senior Selection Secretary, Ministry Division. Bishop Wilfred Wood, Bishop of Croydon (first black bishop) retired in 2002.

The diocesan level

1. Through CMEAC's Advisory Team visits, several dioceses are responding to the importance of setting up positive programmes to combat institutional racism. Twelve dioceses have appointed officers specifically to do this work. In 25 dioceses the Diocesan Social Responsibility Officer or the Bishop's Chaplain has that responsibility.

2. The CMEAC Advisory team visits have often led to the diocese making contact the first time with secular agencies engaged in 'race' issues and in some instances this has led to them working collaboratively. Also the

visits have raised awareness among Church policy-makers of what is actually happening in their diocese, in terms of the ethnic make-up and minority ethnic needs.

3. *The Good Practice Paper for Dioceses*, as well as *The Passing Winter* report display good practice in dioceses which it is hoped all dioceses will learn from and adopt appropriately.

4. There is an emerging and genuine concern about the importance of encouraging minority ethnic Anglican vocations. The initiatives being taken by the Diocese of Southwark, the report on 'Vocations' in *Called to Lead*, and CMEAC's *Serving God in Church and Community* have given impetus to this area of work.

5. The Diocesan Network (Joynt Hope and DLPs) is a valuable resource which liaises between the dioceses and the Committee. They are raising awareness of the issues and always prodding the dioceses to take further action.

6. In several dioceses the bishop's staff have undertaken racism awareness training.

7. Black Anglicans are becoming more visible in the life of the Church, e.g. the following canons have been appointed: in the Diocese of Liverpool – Canon Clarry Hendrickse; in Leicester – Canon Irving Richards; and two lay Canons – Canon Justin McKenzie in Chelmsford and Canon Travis Johnson in Ripon and Leeds. The Ven. Danny Kajumba has been appointed Archdeacon of Reigate in Southwark Diocese.

The Church of England needs to make a conscientious and deliberate effort to identify and appoint more minority ethnic people to senior positions in the structures, otherwise the few who are appointed will be perceived as tokens. These appointments need to be seen as the norm and not as the exception. Over the years progress in this respect appears to be incremental.

chapter 24

What more needs to be done?

The national level

1. Equal opportunities and the importance of valuing cultural diversity need to be written into the policies of GS bodies so that they are always reflected in their board/council/committee/working party membership; and work programme. In an endorsement of the *Called to Lead* report the archbishops have said that with respect to 'employment within our national Church institutions ... we would like to build on the equal opportunities work described in para. 15'.[1]

2. GS boards and councils do act in an advisory role to their counterparts in the dioceses. They need to be pro-active in suggesting how those bodies should respond to issues raised in the Stephen Lawrence Inquiry Report and in CMEAC's publications.

3. GS boards and councils must ensure that information and resources reflect the diversity of the Church, and encourage the appropriate use of terminology on 'race' issues.

The diocesan level

1. In my opinion, on the whole the response to combating institutional racism has been good in a few dioceses, maybe well-intentioned but patchy in most. CMEAC's publications (*Seeds of Hope, The Passing Winter, Roots and Wings*, the *Seeds of Hope in the Parish Study Pack, The Good Practice Paper*), as well as reports and recommendations to dioceses arising out of Advisory Team visits, all refer to the importance of an integrated and holistic approach if changes which are brought about are to be sustained. Too often programmes fall flat when a well-meaning and committed person moves on. Strategies need to be integrated into policies, so that the changes become established. My concern here is that the majority of dioceses tend to have a 'pick and mix' approach – they will implement the strategies which are not too challenging, without getting to the heart of the matter.

2. With respect to Equal Opportunities Policy – the Church at every level must ask itself whether at all times its recruitment, training and

promotion policies are fair. EOP is a step-by-step process, it is not a 'band aid' approach.

3. All dioceses, through the parish clergy, need to work at identifying, encouraging and supporting minority ethnic Anglicans who wish to explore vocations. To what extent are clergy helping leadership to emerge?

4. Diocesan boards and councils need to be much more aware of their responsibility on 'race' issues and formulate practical action plans. The Diocesan Boards of Education in rural areas should find the *Valuing Cultural Diversity Report* a very useful resource. Boards of Education in inner-city and urban areas can refer to other resources like *Colour and Spice*, *Respect for All*, and the CRE's publication entitled *Learning for All*.

5. Dioceses which have not acted as yet should set up a programme of racism awareness training for diocesan decision-makers. CMEAC can be consulted on reliable trainers.

6. Dioceses should ensure that clergy and lay ministers in parishes receive training in racism awareness and the importance of valuing cultural diversity. There is still a hard core of parishes which have the attitude 'There are no black people here so there is no problem'. There is a lot of educational work still to be done with the clergy and the parishes. All parishes in the Diocese of London were given copies of the *Seeds of Hope in the Parish Study Pack*. Ninety-eight per cent gave feedback on how the pack was used. A training audit is being planned as a result of what was said.

7. Dioceses which have had Advisory Team visits should work at implementing the recommendations, and not just 'tinker' at the edges.

8. The dioceses will need to work much harder at encouraging minority ethnic Anglicans to stand for GS Elections. The record shows that figures rose from six to fourteen in 1990 and settled there in 1995. In the 2000 GS Elections there was an increase by one to fifteen members. These small numbers impose a burden on the few as they are usually involved in several pieces of work at the national level, as well as responsibilities as representatives of their dioceses. GS minority ethnic members between 1995–2000 and 2000–2005 are attached as Appendices 13 and 14.

An inclusive diocese

An inclusive diocese is one in which:

- the bishop of the diocese takes responsibility for addressing injustice;
- there is ... education on issues of injustice in all congregations and structures of the diocese and ... resource persons are available

(whether through the church or secular agencies) to provide education;

- leadership is shared by a diversity of people on every level of the church;
- evangelism is a strong force and evangelism committees constantly ask the following questions:
  1. Who is not here?
  2. Who is not represented?
  3. How can others be included?
- there is recruitment of minority ethnic clergy in majority ethnic congregations and there is significant and concrete support for congregations who make these choices;
- there is an EOP and conscientious efforts are made to recruit minority ethnic staff, as well as nominate minority ethnic people to serve on boards/councils/committees;
- the liturgy in congregation is understandable and responsive to all. Barriers to inclusion are removed in vocabulary, education and style.[2]

I have attempted to tell the story of the development of the Committee's work in an effort to document the major aspects of its history. In order to influence change in the structures, the Committee had to develop a range of strategies as what was applicable in one setting did not necessarily work in another setting. CMEAC had to be strategic, methodical, focused and true to its mandate. Following up and monitoring took a lot of effort and demanded painstaking application which in the end was rewarding. We had to learn 'to stick with it' despite disappointments. The strength of CMEAC is in its leadership – the Chairmen, the Committee members, the Terms of Reference, the status of the Committee – at the centre of the Church and accountable first to the Standing Committee and then to the Archbishops' Council.

This report *An Amazing Journey* has recorded the development of the work of the Archbishops' Council's Committee for Minority Ethnic Anglican Concerns (former CBAC). The report has been written from a personal perspective so that it would afford me the opportunity of sharing with the reader insights into the Committee's failures and successes. The report has shown the step-by-step process which CMEAC had to develop in order to make an impact on the structures. It has been not only an amazing but also a daunting journey. There has been change and a shift in thinking and action in some parts of the Church of England, at the national level and to some extent at the diocesan level. A great deal more educational work needs to be done at the deanery and parish levels in order to raise people's awareness and understanding of 'race' and racial justice issues. Due to the effort of BSR's Race and Community Relations Committee and its successor body, the Community and Urban Affairs Committee, with each successive year more parishes were commemorating Racial Justice Sunday.

In my interview with Bishop John Gladwin (mentioned earlier in this report), he spoke of the implicit unacknowledged racism, the struggle to get people to understand the dynamics of institutional racism. Some people considered racism as an urban issue, which it was not. He felt that the cultural shift had not happened although the Committee's work had brought about a shift, a consciousness of the issues around the Church. The institutions were resistant to change, and so there was a continuous task to be done with raising awareness. Bishop John remarked, 'in terms of achievements, people forget where we were'.

I have always felt that it is an indictment on the Church of England that such a Committee is needed and really hope that one day in the not too distant future this work will no longer be necessary as the Church would have rid itself of institutional racism. A great deal has been done but there is a great deal more to be done.

If I were to give a school report on the Church of England and its work on combating institutional racism, my comment would be – the Church has improved in its understanding of the issues but needs to work much harder at positively implementing equal opportunities policy at all levels. The Church has to be genuinely committed to sustained efforts in its processes so as to combat institutional racism effectively through its policies and practices; window dressing will not do.

In the Queen's speech, delivered in Westminster Hall before both Houses of Parliament in her Jubilee Year, Her Majesty recognized the demand for change and development in the role both of Parliament as well as of the Monarchy. The Queen rightly remarked 'change has become a constant; managing it has become an expanding discipline. The way we embrace it defines our future'. The Queen went on to say that bodies such as the Monarchy and Parliament 'in turn must continue to evolve if they are to provide effective beacons of trust and unity to succeeding generations'.

In conclusion, the Church of England as the established Church also needs to consider its role in the twenty-first century. As the Church it needs to be constant in its theology and biblical teachings, but as an institution which is present in every corner of England, the Church needs to adapt to change, to be more inclusive in order to reflect the people of God in all their diversity, if it is to truly reflect the kingdom of God on earth.

appendix 1
CBAC's constitution and membership

The recommendations the Synod endorsed for the membership of the Committee were that the Chairman and the majority of members should be from minority ethnic groups, but that they should be truly representative – and be perceived to be truly representative – of the range of opinions within the ethnic minority constituency. Against this background the Committee was to comprise:

1. The Chairman, nominated by the Presidents.
2. Six members appointed by the Standing Committee (to represent that Committee, the Central Board of Finance, the Advisory Council for the Church's Ministry, the Board of Education, the Board for Social Responsibility, and the Board for Mission and Unity).
3. Two representatives of the black Synod members, chosen by themselves.
4. Two representatives of the Association of Black Clergy.
5. Six nominees of the House of Bishops (chosen by the Bishops on the advice of the Urban Bishops and in the light of consultations in their dioceses and elsewhere).
6. Four co-opted members.

At least one of the four black Synod and ABC representatives and at least two of the Bishops' nominees should be Asian: at least three of the Bishops' six nominees and at least two of the co-opted members should be lay.

Members of the Committee on Black Anglican Concerns (1987–1991)

Chairman Rt Revd Dr Wilfred Wood *The Bishop of Croydon

Six Standing Committee nominees representing:

1. ACCM	*Mr M.D. Birchall
2. The Board of Education	*The Ven. J.E. Burgess (The Archdeacon of Bath)
3. The Board for Mission and Unity	*The Revd Canon M.M. Wolfe
4. The Board for Social Responsibility	*The Revd R. Daniel
5. The Central Board of Finance	*The Revd Canon J.H. Williams
6. The Standing Committee	*The Ven. D. Silk (The Archdeacon of Leicester)

Two Representatives of the Black Synod Members:

1. *The Revd Canon I. Smith-Cameron
2. *Mrs M. Swinson

Two Representatives of the Association of Black Clergy:

1. The Revd I. Richards
2. The Revd T. Samuel

Six House of Bishops' nominees:

1. Miss E. Lake
2. The Revd C. Lawrence
3. Mrs E. Pitts
4. The Revd M. Rumalshah
5. The Revd B. Thorley
6. Mr L. Wilson

By 1989, three members had to be replaced: Mrs E. Pitts, The Revd Rumalshah and Mr L. Wilson. Two of them went to live abroad. Miss Yvette Turner, Mr Charles Severs and Mr Travis Johnson were appointed.

Four co-opted members (to be settled by the Committee)

* = member of the General Synod

Letter and press release from Archbishop Runcie to Bishop Wilfred Wood, CBAC's chairman

Press Release

From the Office of
The Archbishop of Canterbury
Lambeth Palace
London SEI 7JU   020 7928-8282

FOR IMMEDIATE RELEASE   06.02.89

Letter

The following letter was sent on Friday, 3 February 1989 by the Archbishop of Canterbury, Dr Robert Runcie, to the Rt Revd Wilfred Wood, Bishop of Croydon. The meeting mentioned took place on 10 February.

> The General Synod's decision yesterday not to give general approval to the draft Synodical Government (Amendment) Measure will, I know, have been a great disappointment to you and all the members of your Committee. This must be particularly so in the light of the overwhelming support the General Synod gave in November last year to the proposal moved by the Archbishop of York that draft legislation should be prepared.

> Yesterday's decision was taken on a vote by Houses and one House voted narrowly against giving general approval. That binds the General Synod – though as you know the other two Houses voted strongly in favour.

> I am writing to you, as Chairman of the Committee on Black Anglican Concerns, to say that the Archbishop of York and I continue to wish to do all we can to assist and support your Committee and its work. I would welcome therefore, particularly in the light of yesterday's

decision, opportunity to meet personally here at Lambeth Palace with you and the members of your Committee.

I hope that such a meeting can take place within the next few days.

The Right Revd The Bishop of Croydon
Chairman
Committee on Black Anglican Concerns

Letter from Mr Deryck Pattinson, Secretary General, to the diocesan bishops

Dear Bishop,

Participation of Black People in Synodical Government

As you know the Chairman of the House of Clergy and the Chairman of the House of Laity of the General Synod with the encouragement of the Archbishops and the General Synod Standing Committee invited all the Chairmen of Diocesan Houses of Clergy and Laity respectively to separate meetings in the autumn. These meetings discussed the importance of seeking to secure a greater level of participation of black people in Synodical structures – with reference particularly to the General Synod elections of 1990, and of using existing structures rather than (say) provision of special seats.

There was a helpful exchange of views at both meetings about ways and means.

The Archbishops and the Standing Committee asked that, as a next step, the issues should be raised in each Bishop's Council. To help with the presentation, I am enclosing notes of both meetings (copies of both have been sent also to all clerical and lay chairmen). You will see that the Lay chairmen discussed election questions in the second part of their meeting (pages 9-14). The Clerical Chairmen committed themselves to a six point programme – see paragraph 6 on page 7.

Arrangements are being made to alert the Church papers to the fact that these two meetings of diocesan Chairmen took place; I cannot however yet say when any public notice will appear.

In the meantime the Committee on Black Anglican Concerns is playing its part in the process. They will be meeting under the Chairmanship of the Bishop of Croydon with the link persons many bishops have already nominated on Saturday 9 December. This meeting has been structured so as to enable discussion of the kinds of detailed action which can, and should, be followed at diocesan level.

I am sending copies of this letter and enclosures to your Diocesan Secretary.

Yours sincerely

W. D. Pattinson
Secretary General

Analysis of 1990 General Synod election of black members

In the General Synod election results, 14 black candidates of a total of 29, were successful, that is, 48 per cent. This can be considered an improvement over the 1985 General Synod results when 5 candidates were successful.

However, if the 1990 results are looked at in the light of the total elected members of 439, then black members would be 3 per cent. A further comparison looking at black representatives in the three Houses would reveal the following:

	Black members	Total	Percentage
Bishops (suffragan)	1	9	11
Clergy	5	183	2.7
Laity	8	247	2.8
*Total Elected	14	439	3

*Does not include Diocesan Bishops, Deans/Provosts, Archdeacons, Service and Prison Chaplains, Dean of Guernsey/Jersey, University Proctors, Religious, First, Second and Third Church Estates Commissioners, Chairman CBF, Dean of Arches and 2 Vicars General.

	Black members	Total	Percentage
Overall Total	14	*574	2.4

*also includes 10 co-opted members.

In two dioceses, the lay polls were topped by black people – Vasantha Ganadoss and Travis Johnson in Southwark and Ripon respectively.

Feedback from link persons in dioceses where black people were not successful reveal that in several instances candidates lost just by a few votes. This means there is hope that some of these people could well get in on by-elections which might come up over the life of the Synod, 1990 – 1995.

In fact, between 1985 – 1990, by-elections led to 5 more black people becoming members, thereby bringing the total to 10 black members in Synod by July 1990. Feedback also reveals that in some dioceses, black candidates were not strongly supported.

The draft Synodical Government (Amendment) Measure GS 866 which was designed to ensure a minimum number of black Anglicans (24) in General Synod was defeated by the House of Laity in February 1989. This means it is not possible to co-opt members. However, if that had been accepted, then immediately there would be a further increase in the number of black members in General Synod 1990 – 1995. The Chairman of CBAC in the 1988 debate on black membership in General Synod had stated how this would work:

> So there is the possibility that after the 1990 elections, in spite of all our efforts, they may still be fewer than 24. Should this happen, our proposal is that from among those who have stood for election, the number necessary to make up 24 should be added to those elected on the basis of the highest votes polled. Please note that these would be additional members, so no one would have been deprived of a place to make room for black members. Any talk therefore of a quota or reserved places is out of place.

> I have heard the view expressed that no special provision should be made for black people and that they should be elected on their merit. Clearly, to those who take this line, merit is something either bequeathed or infallibly recognized by the electorate. So by choosing people who have already stood for elections and polled some votes we are choosing people who have this merit, although obviously not enough of it.

In the 1985 General Synod Elections and subsequent by-elections, black candidates were successful from six dioceses, namely:

Diocese	Name
Birmingham	The Revd Rajinder Daniel
Bristol	Mr Charles Severs
Chelmsford	Mr Vijay Menon
Liverpool	The Revd Clarry Hendrickse
Ripon	Mr Travis Johnson
Southwark	The Revd Canon Ivor Smith-Cameron

In the 1990 Elections, black candidates who were successful were from a wider spread of dioceses:

Diocese	Name
Birmingham	The Revd Eve Pitts
Bristol	Mr Charles Severs
Chelmsford	Mr Vijay Menon
Liverpool	The Revd Clarry Hendrickse
	Mrs Margaret Swinson
London	Mrs Maria Howell
Manchester	Mrs Louise Da Cacodia
	The Revd Pat Taylor
Oxford	Dr Anna Thomas Betts
Ripon	Mr Travis Johnson
St Albans	The Revd Sam Prasadam
Southwark	The Revd Canon Ivor Smith-Cameron
	The Revd Canon John Sentamu
	Ms Vasantha Gnanadoss

During this quinquennium (1990–1995) Miss Josile Munro was successful in a by-election in the London Diocese.

Glynne Gordon-Carter
Secretary
Committee on Black Anglican Concerns   14 November 1990

CBAC's 1990 revised Terms of Reference

The principal tasks of the Committee on Black Anglican Concerns will be to monitor issues arising; or which ought to arise, in the context of the work of the Standing Committee, the Central Board of Finance and the Synod's Boards and Councils, and of the General Synod itself, as far as they have policy implications for minority ethnic groups within the Church and the wider community. The Committee is asked to pursue its work in close collaboration and partnership with the bodies concerned and their staffs, reporting in the first instance to the Standing Committee and, as appropriate, to the General Synod.

Under these terms of reference the work of the Committee would include:

I. monitoring and making recommendations about the issues which arise, or ought to arise, for black Anglicans in the context of the work of Standing Committee, its sub-committees, the Boards, Councils and other Committees of the General Synod, and of the Central Board of Finance;

II. considering the programmes, budgets and structures to the Standing Committee, its sub-committees, the Boards, Council and other Committees of the General Synod and of the Central Board of Finance, and to provide advice and guidance with a view to supporting efforts for racial justice;

III. acting as a support and resource group for black members of the General Synod and its Boards and Councils;

IV. acting as a spur to, and resource point for, similar work in dioceses;

V. assisting the dioceses in developing strategies for combating racial bias within the Church; encouraging them to make the problems of racism a priority concern in their programmes; and to circulate the best analyses of racism – including theological analyses – and other data helpful for information and education;

VI. liaising with the Race and Community Relations Committee of the Board for Social Responsibility and ecumenical and other agencies concerned with the elimination of racial injustice;

VII. providing for the General Synod an Annual Report concerning its work as if it was a subject to the procedure prescribed by S.O. 105.

appendix 7
CMEAC's 1996 revised Terms of Reference

The principal tasks of the *Committee for Minority Ethnic Anglican Concerns (CMEAC)* will be to monitor issues arising; or which ought to arise, in the context of the work of the Standing Committee, the Central Board of Finance and the Synod's Boards and Councils, and of the General Synod itself, as far as they have policy implications for minority ethnic groups within the Church and the wider community. The Committee is asked to pursue its work in close collaboration and partnership with the bodies concerned and their staffs, reporting in the first instance to the Standing Committee and, as appropriate, to the General Synod.

Under these terms of reference the work of the Committee will include:

1. Monitoring and making recommendations about issues which arise, for *minority ethnic* Anglicans in the context of the work of the Standing Committee, its sub-Committees, the Boards, Councils and other committees of the General Synod, and of the Central Board of Finance.

2. Considering the *membership*, programmes, budgets and structures of the Standing Committee, its sub-committees, the Boards, Councils and other Committees of the General Synod, and of the Central Board of Finance, and *providing* advice and guidance with a view to supporting efforts for racial justice.

3. Acting as a support and resource group for minority ethnic members of the General Synod and of its Boards and Councils.

4. *Acting as a stimulus, support and resource point for similar work in diocesan synods and in their Boards and Councils, and monitoring such work.*

5. Assisting the *bishops and their* dioceses in developing *diocesanwide* strategies for combating racial bias within the church; encouraging them to make the problems of racism a priority concern in their programmes, and to circulate the best analyses of racism – including theological analyses – and other data helpful for information and education.

6. *Seeking the development and empowerment of minority ethnic Anglicans, and in particular fostering and encouraging vocations within the Church.*

7. *In collaboration with the Council for Christian Unity, monitoring and strengthening relationships with the Churches with a preponderance of minority ethnic members, and with the minority ethnic agencies of the historic 'mainstream' Churches of this country.*

8. Liasing with the Race and Community Relations Committee of the Board for Social Responsibility and with ecumenical and other agencies concerned with the elimination of racial injustice.

9. Providing for the General Synod Annual Report concerning its work as if it was subject to the procedure prescribed by SO.96

The changes in the Terms of Reference are given in italics.

CMEAC's members 1991–1996

Chairman   The Revd Canon Dr John Sentamu

Standing Committee nominee representing:

1. **The Standing Committee**
The Very Revd David Silk
The Very Revd Robert Jeffrey replaced Archdeacon David Silk

2. **Advisory Board of Ministry**
The Ven. Gordon W. Kuhrt

3. **The Board of Education**
The Revd Canon Peter Boulton
Mrs Gloria Rich replaced Canon Boulton

4. **The Board of Mission**
Mrs Ann Gill

5. **The Board for Social Responsibility**
Mrs Elaine Appelbee

6. **The Council for Christian Unity**
The Rt Revd Colin Buchanan

7. **The Central Board of Finance**
Mr Travis Johnson

Representatives of the black Synod members
Miss Vasantha B.K. Gnanadoss
The Revd Clarry Hendrickse

Representatives of the Association of Black Clergy
The Revd Theo Samuel
The Revd Ivor Morris

House of Bishops' nominees
Miss Cynthia Sutherland
Mrs Vinnette Melbourne
Sister Yvette Poole
The Revd Charles Lawrence replaced Sr Yvette Poole
Mr Charles Severs
Mr O. Justin McKenzie
Dr John Thomas

Co-opted member
The Revd Canon Ivor Smith-Cameron

Consultant
The Rt Revd Dr Wilfred Wood

Recommendations to General Synod from the report *Identity, Integrity and Impact in the Decade of Evangelism* (Afro-Anglicanism conference held in South Africa)

It is of the nature of sinful humanity that frequently we do not live up to our noblest intentions. It is therefore a truism to say that to pronounce apartheid at an end, even in the Church, does not necessarily make it so.

We therefore recommend:

1. That such awareness of these issues as we have within General Synod structures be offered to the Church of the Province of South Africa (CPSA) and especially those of the Board for Social Responsibility (BSR), and that if this is taken up, the Committee on Black Anglican Concerns (CBAC) give a lead in this.

2. That in some form the concept of equal opportunities be raised with the CPSA. There is a real danger that apartheid within the CPSA may be continued by other means because of the disparity between the national groups within the CPSA and the present structures of power, wealth and access to opportunity.

3. That ways and means should be explored of establishing stronger links with the church in South Africa, for instance through exchange programmes. The emphasis would be on providing training in areas which they would identify, for example, training in project management and 'change' management.

4. That possibilities of partnerships with parishes be explored; CMS and USPG be encouraged to explore this partnership.

5. That given the Church of England's outstanding record in education, discussions should be held on assistance, and the support which could be offered, as Southern African pre-school education is an area of great

need and many children are educated in buildings which are unsuitable and without proper resources.

6. That there are lessons for the Church of England from the richness of gospel and culture which was evident in Africa and echoed in all our experiences of worship.

7. That discussions should be held with the Anglican church in South Africa in order to ascertain whether assistance is needed and the type of assistance which would be required to assist clergy in townships, as we were told that this is an area of concern as some were unpaid, or lived from hand to mouth.

8. That discussions should be held between the appropriate British government agency and the South African government in order to ascertain what help could be given to townships.

List of CMEAC's Advisory Team visits to dioceses

Bath and Wells
Birmingham
Blackburn
Bradford
Bristol
Carlisle
Chelmsford
Chester
Chichester
Coventry
Derby
Durham

Exeter
Gloucester
Guildford
Hereford
Leicester
Lichfield
Lincoln
Liverpool
London × 2
Manchester
Newcastle
Norwich

Oxford
Peterborough
Portsmouth
Ripon and Leeds
St Albans
Salisbury
Sheffield
Southwark
Southwell
Wakefield
Winchester
York

To be visited:

Canterbury
Ely
Europe
Rochester
Sodor and Man
St Edmundsbury and Ipswich
Truro
Worcester

The Race Relations (Amendment) Act 2000

Like the Human Rights Act 1998, the new Act defines a public authority very widely. Anyone whose work involves functions of a public nature must not discriminate on racial grounds whilst carrying out these functions. This means that all the functions of public authorities, such as central and local government, the Police and NHS, will be subject to the Race Relations Act. The Act will also apply to any private or voluntary agency carrying out any public functions such as running schools, prisons or immigration detention centres, enforcing parking controls or providing residential care. All such activities must be free of racial discrimination.

Section 19B (1) of the Race Relations Act 1976 as amended prohibits discrimination by a public authority in the exercise of any of its functions. Section 19 (B) (2) defines a 'public authority' as any person certain of whose functions are functions of a public nature, fall within the scope of the prohibition of discrimination in section 19B (1). *However, in relation to employment and the provision of certain services such as education and housing the Church, and the various institutions it supports, have always been covered by the original Race Relations Act 1976, and this continues to be the case.*

The positive duty to promote racial equality in section 71 of the Race Relations Act 1976 as amended applies to the governing bodies of all Church of England schools maintained by the local education authority.

It is the CRE's view that all other activities of the Church e.g. marriage and funeral rites are outside the scope of the Race Relations Act 1976 as amended as they are probably not functions of a public nature nor a facility or a service under section 20 of the Act.

The authority for this is the case of Regina v Entry Clearance Officer, Bombay ex parte Amin which held that section 20 applies only to acts which are at least similar to acts that could be done by private persons.

Although the 1976 Race Relations Act states that all public authorities must observe the Act in relation to their employment practices and their activities in the areas of education, housing and the provision of goods, facilities and services; the important change is that under the amended Race Relations Act, it will be unlawful for any public authority to discriminate on racial grounds – directly or indirectly by victimisation – in carrying out any of its functions.

What this means in practice is that public bodies will need to look at all aspects of their work, what they do when they serve and whom they employ and ask how it affects racial equality?
(CRE's reply to a question from CMEAC's Secretary re. the impact of the Act on the Church of England)

CMEAC's Secretary – job description

JOB TITLE:	Secretary, Committee for Minority Ethnic Anglican Concerns
RESPONSIBLE TO:	Mr Richard Hopgood, Director of Policy
RESPONSIBLE FOR:	Personal Secretary
GRADE:	Senior Executive Officer

Main Purpose of Job:

To support and develop the work of the Committee in challenging the Church to effectively combat racism in its systems and institutions.

Principal Tasks:

1. To work closely with the Chairman and to carry out work agreed by the Committee.

2. To advise the Committee on the development of its work with respect to its task of monitoring issues arising, or which ought to arise in the context of the work of the Archbishops' Council, GS Boards and Councils, and of the GS itself as far as they have policy implications for minority ethnic groups within the Church, and the wider community.

3. To advise the Committee on all substantial issues affecting the needs and concerns of minority ethnic Anglicans.

4. To support actively and assist the Committee in resourcing the work of dioceses in their task of combating racism.

5. To assess the priorities of the Committee's work in the light of the work of the Community and Urban Affairs Committees (CUAC) and GS Boards and Councils.

6. To establish good working relationships with other churches, agencies and institutions committed to the task of combating racism and racial injustice, including the black majority churches.

Duties:

1. To prepare agendas, minutes, papers and correspondence for Committee meetings.

2. To identify critical issues and to help in finding Christian responses to them.

3. To develop and present to the Committee an Annual Review and a Forward Plan for discussion and decision.

4. To organize and conduct research on behalf of the Committee as necessary.

5. To manage the Committee's programme of work and be responsible for servicing working parties, sub-committee meetings, organizing Conferences and other special events.

6. To design Project Proposals and to develop and manage projects.

7. To develop efficient systems and ensure proper management of the office and its work.

8. To work collaboratively with staff of GS Boards and Councils, in order to encourage them to consider strategies against racism as an integral part of their agenda.

9. To represent the Church of England at Conferences and other events as required; this often includes the presentation of papers.

10. To further develop and support the CMEAC Diocesan (DLPs) and the Joynt Hope network through the bi-annual meetings, regular mailings and Diocesan visits.

11. To support minority ethnic members of General Synod.

12. To support diocesan initiatives and strategies which are being undertaken in response to *Seeds of Hope*, *The Passing Winter* and the *Seeds of Hope in the Parish Study Pack* at all levels of the Church by responding to requests for assistance by way of advice, resource materials, information, speakers and visits.

13. To report to the Director of Policy as necessary.

14. To liaise and collaborate regularly with the Secretary of CUAC.

15. To laise with the Principal of the Simon of Cyrene Theological Institute.

16. To attend GS Senior Staff meetings as practicable and contribute positively to the development of the GS's work.

- Since October 1998, my responsibility for staff has included supervision of an intern. Added to that I am serving as Line Manager to the Researcher who has been employed to conduct the Minority Ethnic Anglican Youth Research Project.

July 2000

General Synod minority ethnic members 1995–2000

Diocese	Names
Birmingham	Dr Raman Bedi
	The Revd George Kovoor
	The Revd Eve Pitts
Canterbury	Mrs Naomi Lumutenga
Liverpool	Mrs Margaret Swinson
London	Ms Josile Munro
Manchester	Mrs Louise Dacocodia
Newcastle	Mrs Hazel Simmons
Oxford	Dr Anna Thomas-Betts
	Mrs Beverley Ruddock
Ripon	Ms Dorothy Stewart
Rochester	The Rt Revd Dr Michael Nazir-Ali
Southwark	Miss Vasantha Gnanadoss
	The Revd Jennifer Thomas

General Synod minority ethnic members 2000–2005

Diocese	Name
Birmingham	The Revd George Kovoor
Bradford	Mrs Zahida Mallard
Canterbury	Mrs Naomi Lumutenga
Coventry	The Revd Canon Andrew White
Liverpool	Mrs Margaret Swinson
London	Ms Josile Munro
	The Revd Simon Pothen
Oxford	Mrs Beverley Ruddock
	Dr Anna Thomas-Betts
Ripon and Leeds	Mrs Dorothy Stewart
Southwark	Mrs Pat Dyer
	Ms Vasantha Gnanadoss
	The Revd Jennifer Thomas
St. Albans	Professor Raman Bedi

Bishop Michael Nazir-Ali, Bishop of Rochester Diocese will also be serving in his role as a diocesan bishop.

CMEAC members 1996–2001

Chairman
The Rt Revd Dr John Sentamu
The Revd Rose Hudson-Wilkin succeeded Bishop John Sentamu
who resigned in July 1999

Standing Committee
Mr Trevor Stevenson
In 1999 the Archbishops' Council replaced the GS Standing Committee.
The Council's representative on CMEAC was the Revd Canon Hugh Wilcox

Appointments Committee
The Committee's representative on CMEAC was Mrs Christina Rees

Board of Education
Mr Geoffrey Locke

Board of Mission
Mrs Christine McMullen

Advisory Board of Ministry
The Revd Canon David Gillett
The Revd Dr Francis Bridger replaced Bishop Gillett towards the end of this
term

Central Board of Finance
Canon Anthony Robinson
His appointment as Archdeacon of Pontefract during this term left a vacancy

Council for Christian Unity
Mr Frank Knaggs

Board for Social Responsibility
Mrs Julia Flack

*The Association of Black Clergy
The Revd Prebendary Theo Samuel
The Revd Ivor Morris

Minority ethnic Synod members
Mrs Dorothy Stewart
The Revd George Kovoor

House of Bishops' representative
The Rt Revd Colin Buchanan

House of Bishops' nominees
The Revd Charles Lawrence
Mr Deo Meghan
The Revd Jonas Mdumulla
Ms Smitha Prasadam
Mrs Beverley Ruddock

Co-opted members
The Revd Canon Clarry Hendrickse
Mrs Gloria Rich

Consultant to the Committee
The Rt Revd Dr Wilfred Wood

*The Association of Black Clergy
The Revd Tunde Roberts
The Revd Dr Olubunmi Fagbemi

CMEAC members 2001–2005

The Chairman
The Revd Rose Hudson-Wilkin

The Archbishop's Council
The Revd Canon Hugh Wilcox

The Appointments Committee
Ms Jayne Ozanne

Board of Education
Mr Stuart Emmason

Ministry Division
The Revd Dr Francis Bridger

Board of Mission
To be appointed

Council for Christian Unity
To be appointed

Board for Social Responsibility
The Revd Anthony Braddick-Southgate

Minority ethnic Synod members
Mrs Dorothy Stewart
The Revd George Kovoor

The Association of Black Clergy
The Revd Canon Tunde Roberts
The Revd Dr Olubunmi Fagbemi

House of Bishops' representative
The Rt Revd John Austin

House of Bishops' nominees
The Revd Simon Pothen, also Deputy Chairman
Mrs Carmen Franklin
Mrs Zahida Mallard
The Revd Jonas Mdmulla
Mrs Beverley Ruddock

Co-opted members
Mrs Christina Rees
To be appointed

Consultant to the Committee
To be appointed

Bibliography

African Caribbean Elders Society (ACES), *Cold Arrival: Life in a Second Homeland*, Print and Design Centre, 1996.

Anglicans and Racism: The Balsall Heath Consultation 1986 Address, Reports and Recommendations, The Church of England Board for Social Responsibility's Race, Pluralism and Community Group, 1986.

F. R. Augier, S. C. Gordon, D. G. Hall and M. Reckord, *The Making of the West Indies*, Longmans, 1960.

Black Catholics Speak, Reflections on Experience, Faith and Theology, Catholic Association for Racial Justice, 1991.

Black Theology in Britain: A Journal of Contextual Practice, issue 4, 2000.

Britain as a Multi-Racial and Multi-Cultural Society, GS 328, Church Information Office, 1977.

Call to Order: Vocation and Ministry in the Church of England, the report of a Working Party, ACCM, Central Board of Finance of the Church of England, 1989.

Called to Lead: A Challenge to Include Minority Ethnic People, a report by the Stephen Lawrence Follow-up Staff Group, GS Misc 625, The General Synod of the Church of England, 2000.

The Church of England and Racism, The Church of England Board for Social Responsibility, Leicester Consultation (81) 40, 1981.

The Church of England and Racism and Beyond, The Church of England Board for Social Responsibility's Race, Pluralism and Community Group, 1982.

Commission on the Future of Multi-Ethnic Britain, *The Future of Multi-Ethnic Britain,* The Parekh report, Runnymede Trust, Profile Books, 2000.

Judith Conley and the Revd Charlie Virga, *Workbook for the Dream Works: Methodology for Changing Oppressive Systems*, ECUSA.

Helen Derbyshire, *Not in Norfolk: Tackling the Invisibility of Racism*, Norfolk and Norwich Race Equality Council, 1994.

V. Dozier, *The Dream of God: A Call to Return*, Cowley Publications, 1991.

Ethnic Minorities in Britain: Diversity and Disadvantages, The Fourth National Survey of Ethnic Minorities, The Policy Studies Institute, 1997.

Faith in the City: A Call for Action by Church and Nation, the report of the Archbishop of Canterbury's Commission on Urban Priority Areas, Church House Publishing, 1985.

Faithful and Equal, report adopted at the Portsmouth Methodist Conference, Peterborough Methodist Publishing House, 1987.

Peter Fryer, *Staying Power: The History of Black People in Britain,* Billing and Sons Ltd, 1984.

The Future of Multi-Ethnic Britain, Runnymede Trust Report, Profile Books Ltd, 2000.

M. Galton and L. Hargreaves, 'Valuing cultural diversity in rural primary schools', final report of a pilot project, 1999.

S. Goodridge, S. Parsons and R. Richardson (eds), *Facing the Challenge of Racism: Story, Reflection and Practice in Theological Education and Training,* ABM in association with the Runnymede Trust Ministry, Paper No.8, Central Board of Finance of the Church of England, 1994.

Clarence Hendrickse, 'General Synod's response to racism as a factor in the Church of England's maturation as a national Church', M.Phil. thesis, University of Nottingham, 1995.

Clifford Hill, *West Indian Migrants and the London Churches,* Oxford University Press, 1963.

Integration and Assessment, An Interim Evaluation of College and Courses, Responses to ACCM Paper No. 22, report of an ABM Working Party on Educational Practice, ABM Ministry Paper No. 3, Central Board of Finance of the Church of England, 1992.

Sam King, *Forty Winters: Memories of Britain's Post-war Caribbean Immigrants.*

Charles Lawrence, *Structure and funding of the Ordination Training Working Party,* unpublished paper, 2001.

Kenneth Leech, *The Fields of Charity and Sin: Reflections on Combating Racism in the Church of England,* The Board for Social Responsibility's Race, Pluralism and Community Group, 1986.

Living Faith in the City: A Progress Report by the Archbishop of Canterbury's Advisory Group on Urban Priority Areas, General Synod of the Church of England, 1990.

Paul McGilchrist (ed.), *Black Voices, An Anthology of ACER's Black Young Writers Competition*, ACER Centre, 1987.

Minority Ethnic Issues in Social Exclusion and Neighbourhood Renewal: A Guide to the Work of the Social Exclusion Unit and the Policy Action Teams so far, Cabinet Office, 2000.

The New Black Presence in Britain: A Christian Scrutiny, a statement by the British Council of Churches' Working Party on Britain as a Multi-Racial Society, 1976.

J. H. Parry and P. M. Sherlock, *A Short History of the West Indies*, Macmillan and Co. Ltd, 1960.

Pioneers and Pilgrims, USPG Tercentenary 1701–2001, Warners Midlands, 2001.

Recovering the Feather, the First Anglican Native Convocation, Anglican Magazine for Council for Native Ministries, Anglican Church of Canada, 1988.

Report of an Independent Inquiry into Institutional Racism within the Structures of the Diocese of Southwark, 2000.

Barbara Rogers, *Race No Peace Without Justice: Churches Confront Racism of the 1980s*, Programme to Combat Racism, World Council of Churches, Geneva, 1980.

Peter Selby, *Belonging: Challenge to a Tribal Church*, SPCK, 1991.

A. Sivanandan, *A Different Hunger: Writings on Black Resistance*, Pluto Press, 1982.

Ivor Smith-Cameron, *The Church of Many Colours: The Experiences and Reflections of a Senior Minister of the Church of England*, Jeyaram Press, 1998.

The Stephen Lawrence Inquiry, report of an Inquiry by Sir William Macpherson of Cluny, advised by Tom Cook, the Rt Revd Dr John Sentamu, Dr Richard Stone, The Stationery Office Ltd, 1999.

Swann, Lord, *Education for All*, Stationery Office, 1985.

The Scarman Report: The Brixton Disorders 10–12 April 1981, report of an inquiry by the Rt Hon. the Lord Scarman OBE, Her Majesty's Stationery Office.

Richard Skellington, *Race in Britain Today*, Sage, 1996.

Social Exclusion Unit, *Truancy and Social Exclusion*, TSO, 1998.

Theology and Racism 2.

H. Walton, *A Tree God Planted: Black People in British Methodism*, Ethnic Minority in Methodism Working Group, 1995.

J. Wilkinson, R. Wilkinson and J. Evans, *Inheritors Together, Black People in the Church of England, Theology and Racism*, 2, The Church of England Board for Responsibility's Race, Pluralism and Community Group, 1985.

With You in Spirit?, the report of Cardinal Hume's Advisory Group on the Catholic Church's Commitment to the Black Community, 1986.

Committee's Publications

Afro-Anglicanism, Identity, Integrity and Impact in the Decade of Evangelism, report of the Second International Conference on Afro-Anglicanism, General Synod of the Church of England, 1995.

CBAC's and CMEAC's annual reports, 1987–1999.

CBAC's General Synod Election Pack, 1999.

How We Stand, a report on black Anglican membership of the Church of England in the 1990s, General Synod of the Church of England, 1994.

The Passing Winter: A Sequel to Seeds of Hope, Church House Publishing, 1996.

Pre-Celebration Pack for the 1994 Black Anglican Celebration for the Decade of Evangelism, General Synod of the Church of England, 1993 (includes video).

Roots and Wings, report of the Black Anglican Celebration for the Decade of Evangelism, General Synod of the Church of England, 1994.

Seeds of Hope: Report of a Survey on Combating Racism in the Dioceses of the Church of England, General Synod of the Church of England, 1991.

Seeds of Hope in the Parish Study Pack, Church House Publishing, 1996.

Serving God in Church and Community, Vocations for Minority Ethnic Anglicans in the Church of England, Church House Publishing, 2000.

Simply Value Us: Meeting the Needs of Young Minority Ethnic Anglicans, GS Misc. 601, Church House Publishing, 2000.

A Good Practice Paper for Dioceses, GS Misc 655, 2001.

Other resources

Colour and Spice, Guidance on Combating Racism in Church Schools, Southwark Diocesan Board of Education, revised edn, 2000.

D. Griffith and D. Lankshear, *Respect for All: Developing Anti-Racist Policies in a Church School,* The National Society of the Church of England, 1996.

David Haslam, *Race for the Millennium: A Challenge to Church and Society,* Church House Publishing, 1996.

Learning for All: Standards for Racial Equality in Schools, The Commission for Racial Equality, 2000.

Making a Positive Difference: Facing the Challenge of Racism and Race Relations: A Study Guide in Five Sessions, Committee for Racial Justice Office, The Methodist Church, 2001.

Racial Justice Sunday Pack, Churches' Commission for Racial Justice (annual publication).

I. Smith-Cameron, *New Lamps: Fresh Insight into Mission: In Celebration of the Ministry of Ivor Smith-Cameron,* Zion Publishers, 2001.

Strangers no More: Transformation through Racial Justice, a training resource, The Methodist Church, 2001.

Valuing Cultural Diversity: A Self-Evaluation Kit for Schools, available from the National Society.

W. Wood, *Keep the Faith Baby: A Bishop Speaks on Faith, Evangelism, Race Relations and Community,* The Bible Reading Fellowship, 1994.

Notes

acknowledgements

1 Board for Social Responsibility Race Relations Field Officer's job description.

2 Kenneth Leech, *The Fields of Charity and Sin: Reflections on Combating Racism in the Church of England*, The Board for Social Responsibility's Race, Pluralism and Community Group, 1986.

summary

1 Job Description: Secretary to RCRC, 1987.

2 Job Description: Secretary to the Committee on Black Anglican Concerns, 1987.

3 *Faith in the City: A Call for Action by Church and Nation*, the report of the Archbishop of Canterbury's Commission on Urban Priority Areas, Church House Publishing, 1985, para. 5.62.

chapter 1 Background

1 A. Sivanandan, *A Different Hunger: Writings on Black Resistance*, Pluto Press, 1982, p. 4.

2 Reference to *The New Black Presence in Britain* in Clarence Hendrickse, 'General Synod's response to racism as a factor in the Church of England's maturation as a national Church', M. Phil. Thesis, University of Nottingham, 1995.

3 F. R. Augier, S. C. Gordon, D. G. Hall and M. Reckord, *The Making of the West Indies*, Longmans, 1960, chapter 7, p. 67.

4 J. H. Parry and P. Sherlock, *A Short History of the West Indies*, Macmillan and Co. Ltd, 1960, pp. 246–8.

5 *Pioneers and Pilgrims, USPG Tercentenary 1701–2001*, Warners Midlands, 2001, p. 4.

6 Augier, Gordon, Hall and Reckord, *The Making of the West Indies*, chapter 12, p. 139.

7 Augier, Gordon, Hall and Reckord, *The Making of the West Indies*, chapter 12, p. 140.

8 Peter Fryer, *Staying Power: The History of Black People in Britain*, Billing and Sons Ltd, 1984, pp. xi, 1, 72–3.

chapter 2 Post-war Britain

1 Fryer, *Staying Power*, pp. 373–4.

2 Fryer, *Staying Power*, pp. 373–4.

3 Clifford Hill, *West Indian Migrants and the London Churches*, Oxford University Press, 1963.

4 Peter Selby, *Belonging: Challenge to a Tribal Church*, SPCK, 1991, pp. 2–3.

5 Selby, *Belonging*, p. 9.

6 Selby, *Belonging*, p. 9.

7 Selby, *Belonging*, p. 10.

8 Selby, *Belonging*, pp. 14–15.

9 Verna Dozier, *The Dream of God*, Cowley Publications, 1991, pp. 1–3.

chapter 3 *Faith in the City: A Call for Action by Church and Nation*
1 *Faith in the City*, para. 5.55.
2 *Faith in the City*, paras 5.57 and 5.58.
3 *Faith in the City*, paras 5.60 and 5.61.

chapter 4 The Committee on Black Anglican Concerns
1 *Faith in the City*, para. 5.74.
2 Excerpts from Bishop Wilfred Wood's speech to the General Synod within his capacity as Chairman to CBAC, November 1988.
3 *Faith in the City*, para.5.74.
4 Hendrickse, 'General Synod's response to racism', p. 295.
5 The reader can consult the following papers in order to get a better understanding of the issues related to the Measure and the advice given by Counsel: 'Black Membership in the General Synod'. Tenth Notice Paper, November 1988; *Black Membership in the General Synod: A Report by the Standing Committee*, GS 844; *Black Membership in the General Synod: A Report by the Committee on Black Anglican Concerns*; Canon Hendrickse's thesis entitled 'General Synod's Response to Racism as a Factor in the Church of England's Maturation as a National Church'.
6 Hendrickse, 'General Synod's response to racism', p. 306.
7 Hendrickse, 'General Synod's response to racism', pp. 307–8.
8 The reader can consult the Church of England Record Centre for the speeches at both debates or Hendrickse's thesis for a summary.
9 *Living Faith in the City: A Progress Report by the Archbishop of Canterbury's Advisory Group on Urban Priority Areas*, General Synod Office of the Church of England, 1990, para 7.6.
10 *Living Faith in the City*, paras 7.6–7.7.
11 *Living Faith in the City*, p. 40.
12 CBAC's General Synod Election Pack, 1999.
13 *Seeds of Hope: Report of a Survey on Combating Racism in the Dioceses of the Church of England*, General Synod of the Church of England, 1991, paras 4.1–4.6.

chapter 5 *Seeds of Hope*
1 Bishop John Sentamu, Message in *Seeds of Hope: Report of a Survey on Combating Racism in the Dioceses of the Church of England*, General Synod of the Church of England, 1991, p. i.
2 Bishop Wilfred Wood, Foreword to *Seeds of Hope*, p. vii.
3 *Seeds of Hope*, p. 1.

chapter 6 Contact with the Church in North America
1 Report of North American visit.

chapter 8 The 1994 Black Anglican Celebration for the Decade of Evangelism
1 George Carey, Archbishop of Canterbury, giving his key note address entitled 'An inclusive liberating gospel' at the 1994 Black Anglican Celebration for the Decade of Evangelism.
2 Archbishop John Habgood, Archbishop of York, delivering his speech entitled 'The gospel and secular England' at the 1994 Black Anglican Celebration.

3 Canon John Sentamu (CBAC's Chairman), commenting at the press conference to launch the Celebration.

4 Charter, Congress of Black Catholics, July 1990, reproduced in *Black Catholics Speak, Reflections on Experience, Faith and Theology*, Catholic Association for Racial Justice, 1991, p. 7.

5 Quotation from the pre-Celebration pack.

6 *Annual Report*, CBAC, 1994, p. 1.

7 *Roots and Wings*, report of the Black Anglican Celebration for the Decade of Evangelism, General Synod of the Church of England, 1994, p. 104.

8 *Annual Report*, CBAC, 1995, p. 3.

9 *Annual Report*, CMEAC, 1995, p. 2.

10 *Roots and Wings*, p. 16.

11 *Common Worship: Services and Prayers for the Church of England*, Church House Publishing, 2000, p. x.

12 Pre-Celebration pack for the 1994 Black Anglican Celebration for the Decade of Evangelism, General Synod of the Church of England, 1993.

13 The Rt Revd John Perry, Bishop of Chelmsford, General Synod debate on *The Passing Winter: A Sequel to Seeds of Hope*, November 1996.

chapter 9 *How we Stand*

1 Introduction to the survey questionnaire.

2 *Faith in the City*, para. 5.68.

3 Archbishop George Carey, General Synod, July 1999 debate on the Church's response to the Stephen Lawrence Inquiry Report.

4 *The Passing Winter: A Sequel to Seeds of Hope*, Church House Publishing, 1996, paras 4.13–4.16.

5 The Revd Ian Stubbs (Manchester) at the 1996 General Synod debate on *The Passing Winter*.

6 Revd Lorraine Dixon, 'A reflection on black identity and belonging in the context of the Anglican Church in England: A way forward', in *Called to Lead: A Challenge to Include Minority Ethnic People*, a report by the Stephen Lawrence Follow-up Staff Group, GS Misc 625, The General Synod of the Church of England, 2000, p. 33. Dixon's article was originally published in *Black Theology in Britain: A Journal of Contextual Praxis,* issue 4, 2000, p. 30.

chapter 10 The development of the Diocesan Network

1 The Trumpet Call, final statement of the 1994 Black Anglican Celebration for the Decade of Evangelism, The General Synod of the Church of England, 1994.

chapter 11 The development of CMEAC's youth work

1 *Simply Value Us: Meeting the Needs of Young Minority Ethnic Anglicans*, GS Misc 601, Church House Publishing, 2000, pp. 29, 34, 43, 44.

2 *Simply Value Us*, p. 1.

chapter 12 The development of vocations

1 'Summary of conclusions for the Minority Ethnic Teaching Consultation', St Albans and Oxford Ministry Course.

2 *Report of an Independent Inquiry into Institutional Racism within the Structures of the Diocese of Southwark,* 2000, para. 4.4.1.

3 Ms Smitha Prasadam, CMEAC Vocations Conference, quoted in *Serving God in Church and Community: Vocations for Minority Ethnic Anglicans in the Church of England,* Church House Publishing, 2000, p. 25.

4 Extract from 'The fourth story, inheritors together', *Theology and Racism* 2.

5 Mrs Margaret Sentamu, 'A possible strategy for nurturing vocations among minority ethnic Anglicans', June 2001.

chapter 13 Asian Anglican concerns
1 Provisional report of the Conversion Conference presented to CMEAC.

chapter 14 *The Passing Winter* and the *Parish Study Pack*
1 Comment by minority ethnic person, 'Report of an Independent Inquiry into Institutional Racism within the Structures of Southwark Diocese', 2000, para. 4.2.1.

2 The Archdeacon of Sheffield, the Ven. Stephen Lowe, now Bishop of Hulme, General Synod debate on *Seeds of Hope,* November 1991.

3 Mrs Elizabeth Fisher, General Synod debate on *The Passing Winter,* November 1996.

4 The Rt Revd John Perry, Bishop of Chelmsford, General Synod debate on *The Passing Winter,* November 1996.

5 *The Passing Winter,* Church House Publishing, 1996, para. 1.10.

6 Rt Revd John Sentamu, General Synod debate on *The Passing Winter,* November 1996.

7 *Annual Report,* CMEAC, 1997, p. 4.

8 *The Seeds of Hope in the Parish Study Pack,* Church House Publishing, 1996, p. 1.

9 *Annual Report,* CMEAC, 1996, p. 10.

chapter 15 *The Passing Winter* Advisory Team visits to dioceses
1 The Bishop of Derby, letter sent to CMEAC's Secretary after the Advisory Team's visit to Derby.

2 The Bishop of Norwich, letter sent to CMEAC's Secretary after the Advisory Team's visit to Norwich.

3 Canon Clarry Hendrickse, Chairman of CMEAC's *The Passing Winter* Advisory sub-Committee, Message in the *Good Practice Paper,* 2001, p. 6.

4 The Revd Rose Hudson-Wilkin, Chairman of CMEAC, Introduction to the *Good Practice Paper,* p. 4.

5 'Racism in rural areas' from the *Good Practice Paper,* pp.32–6.

6 'Continuing ministerial education' from the *Good Practice Paper,* p. 42.

7 'Origin' from the *Good Practice Paper,* pp. 9–10.

chapter 16 Equal Opportunities Policy (EOP)
1 *Called to Lead: A Challenge to Include Minority Ethnic People.* A report by the Stephen Lawrence Follow-up Staff Group, GS Misc 625, The General Synod of the Church of England, 2000, p. 9.

2 Canon Tony Robinson (now Archdeacon of Pontefract), General Synod debate on *The Passing Winter,* November 1996.

chapter 17 Ethnic monitoring

1 Ms Vasantha Gnanadoss, proposer of the motion to include the ethnic origin of members in the revision of the electoral rolls in 2002, General Synod November 2000.

2 Bishop Tom Butler, Southwark Diocese

3 The Rt Revd David Sheppard, Bishop of Liverpool, General Synod debate on *Seeds of Hope*, November 1991.

4 'To the Church of England and its leadership', The Trumpet Call, the final statement of the Black Anglican Celebration, published in *Roots and Wings,* report of the Black Anglican Celebration for the Decade of Evangelism, The General Synod of the Church of England, 1994, p. 5.

5 Barbara Rogers, *Race No Peace Without Justice: Churches Confront Racism of the 1980s*, World Council of Churches, 1980, p.11.

6 Canon Jim Wellington, Leicester, the Stephen Lawrence Inquiry General Synod debate, November 2000.

chapter 18 Valuing cultural diversity

1 M. Galton and L. Hargreaves, *Valuing Cultural Diversity in Rural Primary Schools*, unpublished research report, 1999, p. 42.

2 'Evaluating education inclusion', OFSTED, 2000.

3 Stephen Lawrence Inquiry Report, The Stationery Office Ltd, 1999.

4 Helen Derbyshire, *Not in Norfolk: Tackling the Invisibility of Racism,* Norfolk and Norwich Race Equality Council, 1994.

5 Galton and Hargreaves, *Valuing Cultural Diversity*, p. i.

6 Galton and Hargreaves, *Valuing Cultural Diversity*, p. i.

7 Galton and Hargreaves, *Valuing Cultural Diversity*, pp. 38–9.

8 Galton and Hargreaves, *Valuing Cultural Diversity*, pp. 41–2.

chapter 19 Support for majority ethnic clergy

1 *Report of an Independent Inquiry into Institutional Racism within the Structures of the Diocese of Southwark*, 2000, p. 48.

2 *Called to Lead: A Challenge to Include Minority Ethnic People*, a report by the Stephen Lawrence Follow-up Staff Group, GcIS Misc 625, The General Synod of the Church of England, 2000, para. 65.

3 Galton and Hargreaves, *Valuing Cultural Diversity*, unpublished research report, 1999, p. 41.

4 'Integration and assessment: report of an ABM Working Party on educational practice', ABM Ministry Paper No. 3, March 1992, quoted in *Race in Theological Education: An Audit for use by Colleges and Courses*, p. 84.

5 Revd Dr B. Russell, 'A personal response to equal partners', paper presented at CRRU conference in response to Paul Grant and Raj Patel, *Equal Partners: Theological Training and Racial Justice? Recommendations to Colleges and Boards*, British Council of Churches, 1992.

6 Charles Lawrence, *Structure and funding of the Ordination Training Working Party*, unpublished paper, 2001, p. 1.

chapter 20 The Church of England's response to the Stephen Lawrence Inquiry Report

1 *The Stephen Lawrence Inquiry Report,* The Stationery Office Ltd, 1999, para. 46.27, p. 321.

2 Dr Philip Giddings (Oxford) presenting the report *Called to Lead: A Challenge to Include Minority Ethnic People,* a report by the Stephen Lawrence Follow-up Staff Group, GS Misc 625, The General Synod of the Church of England, General Synod debate, November 2000.

3 Mrs Dorothy Stewart (Ripon and Leeds) General Synod debate, November 2000.

4 Bishop Jim Thompson (Bath and Wells), General Synod debate, November 2000.

5 Appendix 1 of the *Good Practice Paper for Dioceses* has a synopsis of Bishop John Sentamu's paper. The full report is available from CMEAC.

6 Foreword by Sir Herman Ouseley to the *Report of an Independent Inquiry into Institutional Racism within the Structures of the Diocese of Southwark,* 2000.

chapter 21 A different reality

1 'Superiority' by Julie Monica Plenty from Paul McGilchrist, ed., *Black Voices: An Anthology of ACER's Black Young Writers Competition,* Acer Centre, 1987, p. 248.

2 Sam King, *Forty Winters: Memories of Britain's Post-War Caribbean Immigrants.*

3 Gordon, 'Citizenship for some? Government policy 1979–1989', Runnymede Commentary No. 2, April, Runnymede Trust, p. 26, quoted in Richard Skellington, *Race in Britain Today,* Sage, 1996, p. 16.

4 Tariq Modood, Richard Berthoud et al, *Ethnic Minorities in Britain – Diversity and Disadvantage: The Fourth National Survey of Ethnic Minorities,* The Policy Studies Institute, 1997, p. 267.

5 *Social Exclusion Unit Truancy and Social Exclusion,* TSO, 1998, pp. 8–9.

6 *The Future of Multi-Ethnic Britain,* Runnymede Trust Report, Profile Books Ltd, 2000, p. 59.

chapter 22 CMEAC's relationship with the structures

1 The subject of a separate report to the General Synod, *Called to Lead: A Challenge to Include Minority Ethnic People,* a report by the Stephen Lawrence Follow-up Staff Group.

2 The Archbishops' Council's themes for its work 2000–2005.

3 CMEAC paper, 2001/11.

4 *Faith in the City,* pp. 98–9.

5 Letter from Prebendary John Gladwin (BSR's Secretary) to BSR's Chairman, 17 November 1988.

6 Revd Pityana, 'A black Anglican perspective', *Anglicans and Racism: The Balsall Heath Consultation 1986 Address, Reports and Recommendations,* The Church of England Board for Social Responsibility's Race, Pluralism and Community Group, 1986, p. 24.

7 Canon Ivor Smith-Cameron, General Synod 1986.

chapter 23 Future 'Seeds of Hope'?

1 Archbishop of Canterbury, key-note address: 'An inclusive liberating gospel' at the 1994 Black Anglican Celebration.

2 Bishop Peter Selby, 'New languages, new styles, new songs', Presidential Address to Southwark Diocesan Synod, reproduced in S. Goodridge, S. Parsons and R. Richardson (eds), *Facing the Challenge of Racsim: Story, Reflections and Practice in Theological Education and Training,* Advisory Board of Ministry of the Church of England, 1994.

3 Ms Josile Munro (London), General Synod debate on the Stephen Lawrence Inquiry Report, November 2000.

chapter 24 What more needs to be done?

1 *Called to Lead: A Challenge to Include Minority Ethnic People,* a report by the Stephen Lawrence Follow-up Staff Group, GS Misc 625, The General Synod of the Church of England, 2000. Endorsement by the Archbishops (GS 1402) in support of the *Called to Lead* report.

2 Excerpts and adaptations from Judith Conley and the Revd Charlie Virga, *Workbook for the Dream Works: Methodology for Changing Oppressive Systems,* ECUSA, n.d.

Index

Index

EOP Monitoring Group 108, 110
Episcopal Church of the United States of America 45, 46–7, 48–9, 81
equal opportunities policies x, 34, 40, 42, 108–112, 133–4, 153–4, 155–6
ethnicity, ignoring 73, 74
European Ecumenical Assembly, Second (1997) 82
evangelism 55, 58, 67, 85, 155

Fagbemi, Olubunmi 185, 186
Faith in the City 17–19, 20, 45, 194 n.1b
  and black representation in GS 18–19, 21–3, 25–6, 28
  and CBAC xvii–xviii, 143–4
  and combatting racism 51, 141
  and diocesan structures 70, 75
  and ordained ministry 87
  recommendations xi, xiv, 18, 21
Feedback newsletter 77
Fernades, Mavis 52
Ferns, Stephen 89
Fisher, Elizabeth 97, 125, 196 n.3b
Flack, Julia 184
Franklin, Carmen 40, 187
Fraser, Irene 45
Fryer, Douglas 71
Fryer, Peter, *Staying Power* (quoted) 6, 8–9
Future of Multi-Ethnic Britain 137–8

Gadd, Alan 113
Galton, M. and Hargreaves, L. 117, 118–21, 122, 197 n.1b
Gansallo, Ayodele 65
Garlic, David 123
General Synod: and Black Anglican Celebration 65
  black Anglican membership ix, xi, 12–13, 21–9, 32, 66, 154, 161–2, 163–4, 165–7, 182, 183
  Boards and Councils 19, 29–31, 42–3, 50–51, 56, 59, 64, 142, 151, 153, 168, 170
  and *Called to Lead* 132–3, 151
  and CBAC xi, xviii, 18–19, 20–21, 27–8, 34–6, 52
  and CMEAC 97, 151
  and ethnic monitoring 113–14
  and *The Passing Winter* 99–101, 103, 125, 137, 151
  and *Seeds of Hope* 41, 42–3, 44, 58
  and *Simply Value Us* 85
  and Stephen Lawrence Inquiry 115, 130–32
  Young Adult Observer Group 82, 83
  see also Standing Committee
Giddings, Philip x, 115, 129, 132, 198 n.2a
gifts of Black Anglicans 17, 55, 58, 67–9, 75, 85, 87, 116
Gill, Ann 172
Gillett, David 89, 184
Gladwin, John xiv, xv, 40–41, 45, 51–2, 144–5, 156
Gloucester diocese 134
Gnanadoss, Vasantha 111, 113, 165, 167, 172, 182, 183, 197 n.1a
Good Practice Paper for Dioceses 102, 105–7, 152, 198 n.5a
Goodridge, Sehon 32–3
Gordon, (quoted) 136, 198 n.3b
Gordon-Carter, Glynne: and Black Anglican Celebration 66
  and black membership of GS 26–7
  and *Passing Winter* follow-up 104–5
  as secretary of CBAC/CMEAC xvii–xix, 30–31, 39, 50, 53, 145–6, 147–9
  as Secretary to Race and Community Relations Committee xvii, 50, 51–2, 144–5
  and *Seeds of Hope* 41, 44
  and Southwark enquiry into racism 133

and *Valuing Cultural Diversity* project 118
  visit to Church of Scotland 49
  visit to USA and Canada 45–9, 56–7
Granger, Penny 24, 65
Guildford diocese 134

Hall-Wycherley, Nell 65
Habgood, John 23, 24, 27–8, 55, 65, 70, 194 n.2d
Harris, Frank 63
Haslam, David 134
Hasler, Leon 47
Hawkins, Peter 26
Hayden, Carleton 48
Hendrickse, Clarence xiv, 3, 152, 166–7, 172, 185
  General Synod's Response to Racism xiii, xv, 19, 21–2, 24–5, 100, 193 n.2c, 194 nn.4, 6
  and *Passing Winter* Advisory Sub-Committee 103, 105
  and Youth Issues Sub-Committee 80
Hereford diocese 117, 120
Hill, Clifford (quoted) 9–11, 193 n.3c
Hope, David 90
Hopgood, Richard xiv, 132, 179
House of Bishops: and Black Anglican Celebration 64
  and CBAC 20, 158, 159
  and CMEAC 98, 142, 143, 173, 185, 187
  and *Seeds of Hope* 43, 98
  and Stephen Lawrence Inquiry 131
  and Survey of Black Anglicans 70
How We Stand 70–73, 87, 101, 113, 132
Howell, Maria 167
Hudson-Wilkin, Rose xiv, 90, 105–6, 184, 186, 196 n.4c
Human Rights Act (1998) 111, 177

immigration, post-war 3, 8–11
Ineson, Hilary 59

Jackson, David 123
Jacobs, Laverne xv, 45, 49, 56–7
Jeffery, Robert 61, 172
Jenkins, David 40
Johnson, Travis 152, 160, 165, 166–7, 172
'Joynt Hope' 76, 78, 152, 180
justice: and nature of God 31–2
  racial 40, 42, 51–2, 58, 82, 99, 101, 106, 141–2, 154, 169, 170

Kajumba, Danny 152
Kasibante, Amos 33
Khan, Rayman xiv, 61, 82, 86
King, Martin Luther x, xii
King, Sam, *Forty Winters* (quoted) 8, 136
Knaggs, Frank 184
Kovoor, George xiv, 68, 89, 93, 182, 183, 185, 186
Kuhrt, Gordon 88, 89–90, 172
Kwano, Roland 46

Lake, E. 159
Lane, Andrew 134
language and terminology xix, 8, 59, 67, 131, 153
Lankshear, David 118
Lapite, Shijji 138
Lawrence, Charles xiv, 47, 62, 159, 173, 185
  and Vocations Sub-Committee 87–8, 125
Lawrence, Neville 131
leadership, black 18, 25, 33, 46, 58, 150, 155
  and cultural diversity 87, 90, 114–16
  see also vocations
Lee, Gilbert 65
Leech, Kenneth xiii, xix, 51, 52, 147
Leicester Consultation (1981) xiii–xiv, 87
Leicester diocese 60, 71, 116, 152